Baritone Ukulele From Scratch

What every beginner needs to know to get UP and PLAYING as soon as possible, *PLUS*, somewhere to go after that!

☞ *How to Tune your Bari-Uke*

☞ *How to Strum some Simple Chords*

☞ *Our Five Favorite Chord Families*

☞ *Major, Minor and Seventh Chords*

☞ *Plenty of Familiar Song Examples*

☞ *The Magical Circle of Fifths (**BEAD**)*

☞ *Fingerpicking, including Travis-Style*

☞ *Just Enough Music Theory (**CAGED**)*

☞ *Our Favorite Songs All Over the Neck*

☞ *Chords of Color All Over the Neck*

Other Titles by **Bruce Emery:**

Guitar From Scratch series

Guitar From Scratch

Guitar From Scratch: The Sequel

Fingerstyle Guitar From Scratch

Blues Guitiar From Scratch

Travis-Style Guitar From Scratch

Music Principles for the Skeptical Guitarist series:

Volume One: The Big Picture

Volume Two: The Fretboard

Jazz for the Skeptical Guitarist

Christmas Strumalong Guitar

Christmas Fingerstyle Guitar

For teachers:

Guitar From Scratch: Streamlined Edition

More info at: **www.SkepticalGuitarist.com**

Baritone Ukulele From Scratch

by

Bruce Emery

Skeptical Guitarist Publications

© Copyright 2011 Skeptical Guitarist Publications

All rights reserved.

Manufactured in the United States of America

ISBN: 978-0-9788609-2-6

Cover design: Marc Harkness <marc@marcharkness.net>
Webmaster: Lou Dalmaso <loudalmaso@att.net>

Skeptical Guitarist Publications
Post Office Box 5824
Raleigh, NC 27650-5824
(919) 834-2031

Web site: www.SkepticalGuitarist.com
Find audio files and an e-mail link

First Edition

Table of Contents

Introduction and A Look Ahead   1
The Baritone Uke and Me   2
Here We Go   3
Tuning the Bari-Uke   4
Holding and Strumming a G chord   5
Adding the C and D7 chords   8

The G Chord Family   10
   Major, Minor and Seventh chords   11
   Songs in the Key of G   13
   Beyond the 1 - 4 - 5 chords   17
The C Chord Family   21
   Songs in the Key of C   22
The D Chord Family   24
   Songs in the Key of D   25
Patriotic Interlude (3 keys)   27
The A Chord Family   28
   Songs in the Key of A   29
The E Chord Family   30
   Songs in the Key of E   31
Quiz Time for the Chord Families   32
Our 5 Chord Families - Summary   33
The F Chord Family   34
   Songs in the Key of F   35
Full Arrangements in G and C   36
   You Are My Sunshine   36
   Amazing Grace   37
   Sloop John B.   38
   Morning Has Broken   39
   Five Foot Two   40

Circle of Fifths   41
   1st Phenomenon   42
   2nd Phenomenon   43
   3rd Phenomenon   44
   Yuletide Backcycling in G and C   45

Fingerpicking   47
   Arpeggios in 4/4   47
   Arpeggios in 3/4   50
   Travis Picking   52

Scary Theory Part of the Book   55
   C Major Scale   55
   C Chord Family Up the Neck   56
   The Five *C-A-G-E-D* Chord Forms   61
   Big Uke/Small Uke: What's the Dif?   65
   G Chord Family Up the Neck   66
   D Chord Family Up the Neck   69
   Our Three Overlapping Keys   71
   A and E Chord Families Up the Neck   72
   Minor Chords Around the Neck   73

Our Songs All Over the Neck   74
   Amazing Grace (Key of C)   75
   Amazing Grace (Key of D)   76
   Amazing Grace (Key of G)   77
   Morning Has Broken (Key of C)   78
   Auld Lang Syne (Key of D)   80
   Jingle Bells (Key of C)   81
   You Are My Sunshine (Key of D)   82
   Ain't She Sweet (Key of C)   83
   Five Foot Two (Key of C)   84

Beyond the Major and Minor Chords   86
   G Chord Qualities   87
   C Chord Qualities   89
   D Chord Qualities   90
   A and E Chord Qualities   91
   Diminished Chords/F Chords   92
   Rhythm Changes in C, G and D   93
   America the Beautiful in Three Keys   94
Minor Keys   95
   Examples in Am, Em and Dm   96

Intro to Single String Playing   98
Pentatonic Minor Scale   99
Twelve-Bar Blues   100

What Readers of My Other Books Have to Say

Emery is a teacher who apparently has ESP when it comes to learning guitar. Things are broken down into such sensible pieces that you'll wonder why everybody doesn't teach this way. *Recommended!*
Elderly Instruments, Lansing, MI

Thank you for writing something intelligent and witty, something I actually looked forward to reading. Eternal gratitude.
Meredith Cox, Raleigh, NC

I bought your book because it made me laugh.
Mike Schwartz, Montclair, NJ

Send more books! Our customers are eating them like peanuts.
Linda Tillman, McFadyen Music, Fayetteville, NC

Thanks for your warm and friendly style and bits of humorous illustration.
George Demosthenes, New Market, NH

Focused and vastly readable... Conversational approach is warm and engaging...Humor, insight and patience.
David McCarty, Acoustic Guitar Magazine

You are a miracle worker. I'm having the time of my life.
Chuck Slaughter, Cyberspace

The books sell themselves.
David Willmott, Music-Go-Round, Cary, NC

It's written just like you're sitting there teaching me.
Barrett Ferrara, Cyberspace

Your writing is breezy and conversational but still very clear and organized.
Chris Gaskill, Knoxville, TN

You clearly have a real gift, and we're lucky that you put it down on paper
Mark Waite. Houston, TX

There is no better teaching aid on the market than your books. You could write a book on the proper way to put a guitar on a guitar stand and I would buy it! Kevin Johnson, San Antonio, TX

The format is easy on the eyes. Bruce writes in a clear and understandable manner, making it fun to learn.
Ed Benson, Just Jazz Guitar magazine

If you write it, they will buy it.
Paul Miller, New Bern, NC

Bruce, this is an absolutely terrific book. It shows that you have a wonderful sense of humor, a high degree of humility and a great sensitivity to others. A++ and many kudos.
Dick Masom, Tequesta, FL

Bruce Emery has "got it right" with his gentle pace.
Adrian Ingram, Just Jazz Guitar magazine

I can see why people raved about this. This is a great thing you did.
Thomas McLachlen, Pittsburgh, PA

Your content is golden.
Marko Schmitt, Cyberspace

Thanks for getting me fired up! I can play more in 4 weeks than I could after all those years of trying to teach myself.
Kim Lachance, Dover, NH

Your books are greatness because of the enjoyment you experienced while writing them. I was instantly won over by your wit.
Christian Briere, Weatherford, TX

Enjoyable to read; short, to the point and jam-packed full of information.
Lynn Sugg, Winterville, NC

All I can say is YES! Someone has finally hit the nail on the head.
Martin Bell, Staffordshire, England

Introduction and a Look Ahead

I'm Bruce Emery, author of 11 *fascinating* guitar method books,
including the **Guitar From Scratch** and the **Skeptical Guitarist** series.

But my first instrument was the baritone ukulele, and it's been a lot of fun to dust off
my old friend and transfer some of the guitar knowledge I've acquired over the years.
Turns out, it's a much more versatile and complex instrument than I had realized!

Here, I want to give you a preview and offer some guidelines as you go through this thing.

We start off simply, with how to **tune** the bari-uke and how to **strum** some basic chords.
Strumming chords is a good thing to start learning to do right away, and I give you about
a half-dozen strum patterns that you'll be using for the rest of your ukulife.

Learning the rest of the basic chords comes next, and we'll do it by organizing them
into keys, or **Chord Families**, and playing the same familiar songs over and over from
key to key. We like the keys that spell the word "**CAGED**," and we'll be interested
in the **1 - 4 - 5 Major** chords mostly, plus some **Seventh** and **Minor** chords.

There will be some **full arrangements** of our favorite songs, then a discussion
of the Great and Powerful **Circle of Fifths**. Don't worry, it's not as bad as it sounds.
It's actually kind of fun learning about the role that the number **Five** plays in music.
Prepare yourself for some Yuletide Backcycling and BEADing around the bush.
Any of it confusing? **MOVE ON** *to something easier and more fun.*

Then it's on to **Fingerpicking**, first with regular arpeggios and then in the **Travis-Style**,
where an alternating bass creates a ragtime sort of sound. We'll use our same old songs.

The **Scary Theory Part of the Book** is next, the purpose of which is to track down
different forms of our favorite chords all over the neck. *If the analysis starts getting
a bit too hairy, just* **SKIP IT** *and* **learn the chord shapes** *that come out the other side.*

Because next comes **chord-melody** arrangements of **Songs All Over the Neck**,
from *Auld Lang Syne* to *Ain't She Sweet*. Then a discussion of more **Chord Qualities**
(chords of color), with a touch more theory and some help from *America the Beautiful*.

We round things out with an explanation and examples of **Minor Keys** and give
the briefest of introductions to the **Pentatonic Minor Scale** and blues improvisation.

The Baritone Uke and Me

Mom bought herself a little Harmony baritone ukulele back in the 1950s, no doubt inspired by radio and TV personality Arthur Godfrey. I still have that scuffed-up mahogany box. Through the soundhole, you can see what is clearly a *magical* lighthouse beaming out its twilight warning signal over the inscription: "Bruno Means Security." (C. Bruno & Son, Est. 1834, in New York City.)

Mom would actually play the thing; all I did was strum the open strings and gaze dully at that creamy lighthouse, transfixed by those four wispy notes that were being blasted out planet-wide. I was not a musical phenom at the age of four. I did not play any chords, but I *could* eke out most of "Taps" using the 4 open strings. Except that the highest note in the melody---coming about 2/3 of the way through the tune?--- didn't sound right. Who knew that you might actually need to press down a STRING on a FRET to play a song.

But at the ripe old age of nine, I came roaring back to Ukuleleville. Armed with my mother's song books and a surprising dose of ambition, I was all over "Five Foot Two" and "Blue Moon." Early gigs included performing Smothers Brothers routines in the 4th grade and Christmas carols in the 5th. Although I abandoned the uke for the guitar at the age of 12, I must credit my little brown buddy with helping me develop my sense of music.

Though playing the baritone ukulele is a worthy goal in and of itself, it can also serve as a gateway instrument, a stepping stone, to playing the guitar. As it happens: *The four strings of the bari-uke are tuned the same as the first four strings of the guitar.* This is NOT the case with the smaller, more common ukuleles (tenor, concert and soprano).

The guitar is harder to play because of those *two extra strings*, and I often advise the parents of younger guitar aspirants to start with the bari-uke. I believe that the diminutive hands of *this* eager 9-year old were better served by the uke, and that I did *not* suffer from *not* struggling with those two extra strings.

Our Strategy. Once you've learned to **tune** your instrument, we'll jump right into the act of Strumming Chords to Accompany Your Singing Voice. This is probably what 90% of the people who play the uke do with it. I'm not so concerned with giving you the history and culture of the uke, as there are many fine resources that provide such-like.

*I want to give you a practical, technical, nuts-and-bolts intro that will have you playing the bari-uke **intelligently** by your next birthday.*

Here We Go

In the *killer* diagram to the right, you see depicted Your Basic Ukulele.

The strings are tied to the tuners and run through the slots in the nut and down and over the river and across the fretboard and the soundhole, and are tied again to the bridge.

You hold the neck in your left hand and strum the strings with your right hand.

Question: ***Are You Left-Handed?***
If you are, you *still* might want to play the uke right-handed. The practical reason for this is that, since it's a right-handed world (as you are well aware), most of the ukes you will ever run into are strung to be played right-handedly.

You can certainly restring the instrument in reverse order; if you do, you'll need to read the chord diagrams in reverse, but that isn't too great a complication, I suppose.

But really, the two hands perform such different functions that it isn't obvious where to assign the dominant hand. Up to you.

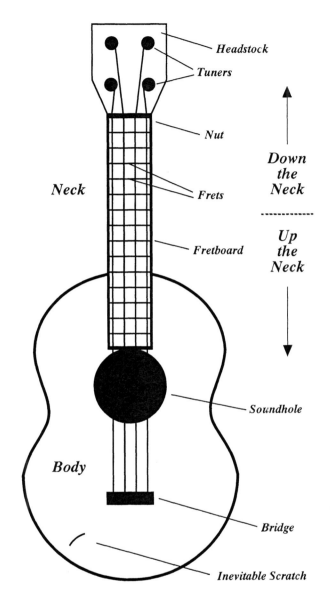

The strings are numbered from 1 to 4, from right to left on the diagram. The 1st and 2nd strings are usually made of clear nylon and the 3rd and 4th strings are made of metal wrapped around, or silverplated onto, a core of nylon filaments. The strings increase in *thickness* and **pitch** (high/lowness) from 1 to 4, so when you hold the uke as a righty, the "highest" string is the one nearest the floor.

Also, the term "up the neck" means toward the soundhole, where the notes sound higher in pitch, and so the nut of the uke is "down the neck." Down the neck is where you'll play your first chords.

Tuning the Bari-Uke: D-G-B-E

First, a word to players of the "Small Ukes." This different tuning for the Big Uke, the **DGBE** tuning, has consequences for you: The chords that you will be learning here will have familiar shapes and fingerings, but they will have *different names*.

So what we call the **G** chord on the Big Uke looks like a **C** chord on the Small Uke. There's a good reason for this, and I'll show you later (page 65) why this is.

. . . .

I'm going to suggest that you go out and buy an electronic tuner. No really, you should get a tuner. Let me put it a different way: A tuner you should get, really.

I'm only thinking of you, Young Uker. Tuning by ear, also known as Relative Tuning, is tricky, especially if your ear for music is still developing. It's better to employ the tuner and be CERTAIN that you are in tune, than it is to throw a Hail Mary pass and hope to land somewhere in the vicinity. Better to hear yourself playing in tune from the start, something I lacked the opportunity to do, coming up through the Thoracic Period.

That being said, I will run you through the process of Relative Tuning, just in case.

So. The diagram to the right gives you a bird's-eye-view. This is a **Fretboard Diagram**, where the dark line on top represents the nut, the vertical lines are the 4 strings, labeled **D - G - B - E** (4th through 1st), and the lower horizontal lines are the first 5 frets.

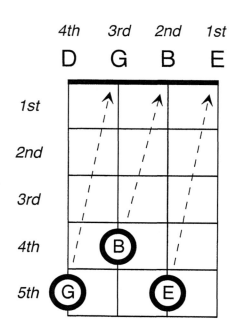

You'll need to get a D note from somewhere (piano or pitch pipe) and tune the 4th string to it as close as you can. Now play the 4th string at the 5th fret, which is a G note, and compare this sound to the open 3rd string, which *also* needs to be a G note. Turn the *3rd-string knob*, start closing the gap between the two pitches, if there is one, and listen for a beating sound that will start to slow down and finally disappear when the notes are "in unison."

Then use the B note at the 4th fret of the 3rd string to get the open B string in tune, and the E note at the 5th fret of the 2nd string to get the open E note in tune. You can also find various tuning sites on something we like to call "The Worldwide Wide Websternet."

Holding and Strumming a G Chord

A chord is a combination of two or more notes that are played at the same time. Sometimes they blend together harmoniously, as **consonant chords**, and sometimes they blend together *less* harmoniously, as **dissonant chords**. And of course there is a whole range of chords from the most consonant to the most dissonant, and what may sound consonant to you may sound dissonant to me.

The **G** chord, which is probably the most common chord and is also among the easiest to play, is perfectly consonant, a very harmonious little chord. You'll see *why* it is called "**G**" in the scary theory portion of the book. The diagram to the right shows that the 3rd finger is holding the 1st string at the 3rd fret and that the 2nd, 3rd and 4th strings are left to ring open (witness the little "O's" on top.) (Apparently a picture is worth about 25 words.) By the way, we don't really distinguish musically between fretted and unfretted notes, regarding them all as equal components of the chords we play. And we usually find ourselves strumming 4-note chords, some of which will have all 4 strings fretted.

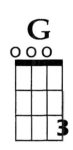

So why is the *3rd* finger used instead of the 1st, 2nd or 4th? One consideration in forming chords is *what other chords* we are likely to visit. For our current purposes, the 3rd finger is the one that allows the easiest access to the chords that are played most frequently with **G**, like **C** and **D7**; you'll see other fingerings for **G** later.

Strumming. I don't think it really matters what tool you use to strum a chord. As a child, I used a floppy felt pick, but nowadays it is more the style to play with the fingers unadorned. Use the Index and/or the Middle Finger to strum **Down** and **Up** with nail and/or skin in either or both directions. You can also work in your Thumb somewhere, either **Down** or **Up**, with nail or skin. But whether you prefer to use a plastic pick, a buffalo nickel or a stale Funyun, I have nothing to say.

Look at the 4 following Down-Up patterns that we will apply to the **G** chord. We'll talk about each of these over the following pages:

D D D D	DUDUDUDU	D DUDUDU	D DU UDU
1 + 2 + 3 + 4 +	1 + 2 + 3 + 4 +	1 + 2 + 3 + 4 +	1 + 2 + 3 + 4 +

By the way, that's called a Tablature Diagram, and usually it displays *numbers* that indicate certain frets on certain strings that you're supposed to play. We'll use it for that later on, but here it's just a way to show Downstrokes and Upstrokes through the passage of time. The passage of time is shown by the "**1 + 2 + 3 + 4 +**" below each **measure**, or **bar**, of music. Each measure has 4 strong beats (the numbers) alternating with 4 weak beats (the plusses). It's called **4/4 Time**, to be counted:
One-and-Two-and-Three-and-Four-and.

So the 1st pattern has 4 strong Downstrokes. Play 4 or 5 measures of this pattern, and wake me when you're through.....Yeah, pretty dull stuff, but you know, sometimes that's the very pattern that works best. Try the 2nd pattern, with the lighter Upstrokes interspersed among the heavier Downstrokes. Juicier, but even that, after a while, begins to sound kinda redundant. And redundant. Specifically, the problem is:
*If you play several measures in a row, it gets harder for your ear to identify the **first beat** (also known as **Count 1**) of succeeding measures.*
All the **Down-Ups** quickly start bleeding together.

The 3rd pattern on the previous page begins to generate some aural interest. It is significant for what's been *left out*: a single Upstroke deleted from **Count 1+** (the "and" note after **Count 1**). This single break in the steady flow of Down-Ups is refreshing, and points directly backward to identify **Count 1** as the **downbeat** of the measure. We'll call this the **Rock Strum Pattern**. Try your **G** chord:

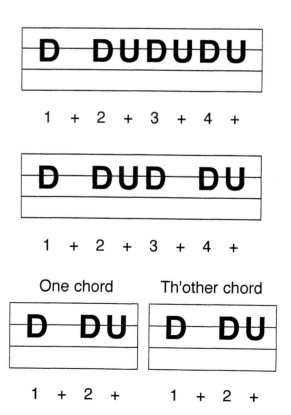

All you're doing is skipping past the strings on the way up after the downbeat. Don't rush. Keep your arm *moving steadily* and don't try to fill in that gap with another fast Downstroke. Let it breathe!

A variation on the Rock Pattern omits *another* Upstroke, the one at **Count 3+**. Your strumming is now brimming with excitement.

But the real value in this variation comes when you *change chords after only 2 beats*, which you will do regularly. It's always best to emphasize a new chord right at the change, so when you make the switch, it's like starting the main pattern over again. Let's call this the **Short Rock Strum Pattern** (2 beats):

Now we'll work with the 4th pattern from two pages back. Like the Rock Pattern, this one lacks an Upstroke on **Count 1+**, but it also lacks a *Downstroke* on **Count 3**. Let's call this the **Folk Strum Pattern**, which sounds breezier than the Rock Pattern:

A bit trickier, with those 2 Upstrokes in a row, which can throw some people. But if you keep your arm *moving steadily*, and resist the temptation to speed up at **Count 3**, you will prevail:

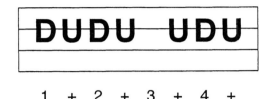

An interesting variation on the Folk Pattern is to *put the Upstroke back in on Count 1+* while keeping **Count 3** unoccupied. And your arm *moving steadily*:

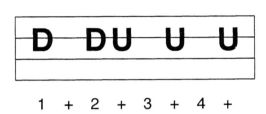

You can also start with the first Folk Pattern and *leave out another Downstroke, at Count 4:* This one sounds the breeziest of all the patterns, especially with your arm *moving steadily*:

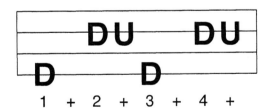

But the take-home lesson on all these strum patterns is to keep your arm moving *relentlessly* **Down** and **Up**, Down on the numbered counts and Up on the "and" counts. This rhythm is the most important thing; just keep the arm swinging and all will be well.

Couple more useful strums to know: first, the **Country Strum Pattern**, where, on **Counts 1** and **3**, you play *only the 4th string as a single bass note,* giving sort of a Boom-chicka, boom-chicka effect:

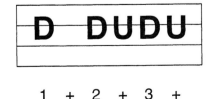

Then the **3/4 Strum**, or **Waltz Strum Pattern**, for songs that have *3 beats per measure instead of the usual 4*. So we have two main **Time Signatures**, named **4/4 Time** when there are 4 beats per measure and **3/4 Time** when there are 3 beats per measure.

You can also do a **Country Waltz Strum Pattern** by playing the 4th string alone on **Count 1**.

Time to learn two new chords, the previously-mentioned **C** and **D7** chords.

The **C** chord has *two* fretted strings and two open strings.
Put your 1st finger (forefinger) at the 1st fret of the 2nd string,
then add the 2nd finger to the 4th string at the 2nd fret,
and be sure to stand both fingers up to avoid
muting the 3rd and 1st strings.

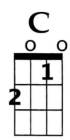

D7 has *three* fretted strings (only one open), and look, one of those
fretted notes, the 1st finger on the 2nd string, *also* appears in the **C** chord.
This is an example of an Anchor Finger, a finger that stays put during
a chord change. The other two fingers fall naturally onto the 3rd and
1st strings at the 2nd fret. I'll explain the "7" in the **D7** later.

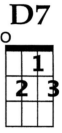

Let's start putting this all together with a **chord progression**
using **G**, **C** and **D7**. Here it is using the Rock Strum Pattern:

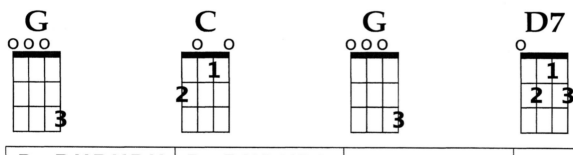

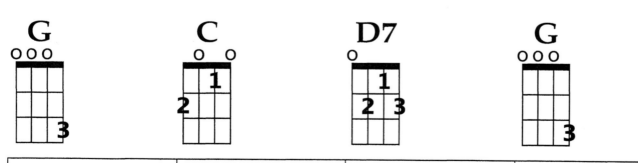

Try the first line again with the Folk Strum Pattern:

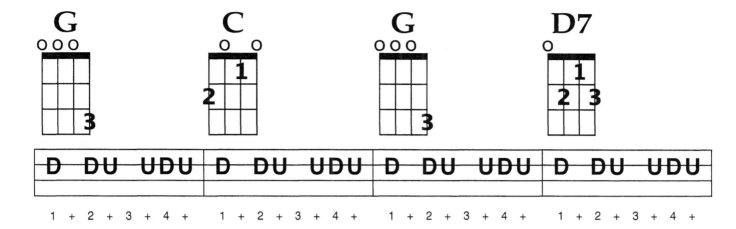

Now with the Country Strum Pattern:

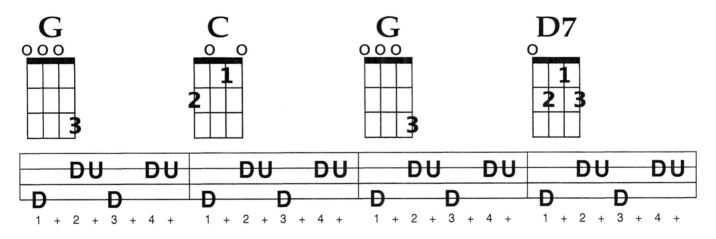

And finally with the Country Waltz Strum Pattern:

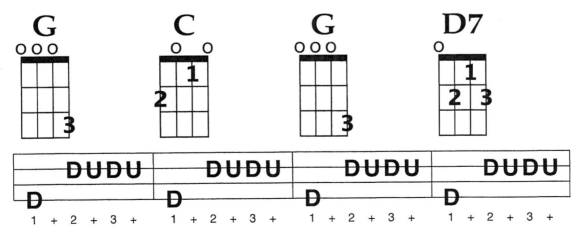

The G Chord Family

Let's dip our collective toe into the cool, invigorating waters of **music theory**. Please believe me when I say that *music theory is the most practical kind of theory in the world*. And I'll show you only the simplest, most useful parts of it, and only as they apply to the ukulele. If you can count to 13, you'll be able to handle anything I shovel at you. You'll feel a gratifying sort of leverage in gaining this knowledge; a little goes a long way, and you will enjoy many "aha!" moments.

You probably already know that the Musical Alphabet contains 7 letters, **A-B-C-D-E-F-G**, and these represent the **natural** notes. And then there are **5 accidental** notes, each known as both a **sharp** (♯) and a **flat** (♭), strewn around in there, too. So there are *12 different notes*, but only 7 letters.

So the 7-note Musical Alphabet repeats over and over, A to G, as we go up in pitch. Here's a portion of the piano keyboard:

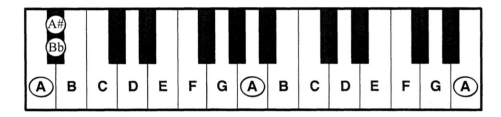

The white keys of the keyboard are the natural notes and the black keys are the accidentals. The black key between the A note and the B note is called either *A-sharp* or *B-flat*, and it goes on like that. When you start counting on an A and travel up the "scale" (*scala* in Latin means ladder) to the next A, you've gone to the *8th letter*, and that's called an **octave**.

That's all we care about individual notes at the moment, except that they can be combined to form CHORDS, and we care *deeply* about chords. After you're comfortable manipulating chords, we'll go back and break them down into their component notes, and the "scales" will fall from your eyes.

So we are going to define a KEY, not as a group of notes, but as a group of *chords* centered around one particular chord, and we'll call this group a **Chord Family**.

The **Key of G**, also known as the **G Chord Family**, consists of a group of chords in which the **G** chord plays a commanding role when all these chords get together in a song. The **G** chord exudes what is known as a **Key Feeling** among these chords. It is the Home Chord. It is Restful. When you are playing in the **Key of G**, **G** is usually the first, last and most frequently played chord.

Each of the 12 notes in music acts as the commanding officer in its own key.
In the **Key of C**, the **C** chord is the boss; in the **Key of D♭**, the **D♭** chord is top dog.
(Also realize that keys overlap, and most chords belong to more than one key.)

Let's look at a handy little **code** for figuring out *which chords belong to which keys*.

Begin by laying out the 7 letters of the Musical Alphabet, **ABCDEFG**, in order,
*but starting with the **Key Note**,* which in this case is **G**. Number them from 1 to 7.
(We will now regard these letters as representing *chords* rather than single notes.)

G	A	B	C	D	E	F
1	2	3	4	5	6	7

Next, pick off the **1st**, **4th** and **5th** letters, which come out to be **G**, **C** and **D**.

In any key, the three biggest chords are the **1 chord**, the **4 chord** and the **5 chord**
in the *Chord Family Line-Up*, so that's **G**, **C** and **D** in the **Key of G**. (For short,
we speak of the **1 - 4 - 5 chords**.) In addition, these three chords possess a

Major Chord Quality

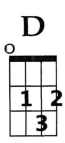

You already know the **G** and **C** chords; here's how to make the **D** chord,
a triangular shape requiring three fingers that looks like a flipped over **D7** chord.
The mighty 2nd finger is not so happy having to sit in the back seat of this chord,
and the shy 3rd finger can be balky when you try to put it into the driver's seat.
Be sure to *arch* the 3rd finger so it doesn't mute out the 1st string.

So what is the connection between the **D** and **D7** chords? The **D** chord,
along with **G** and **C**, is a **Major chord**. We don't usually say "D Major,"
just "D," and assume it's Major. The **D7** chord has a **Seventh Chord Quality**,
and we *do* say "D-seven." But the Seventh chord is *built on* a Major chord,
and just happens to be outfitted with an extra note (more about that later).
So it can substitute for a Major chord for our current purposes.

So, to generalize to all keys: *It is perfectly legitimate for the 5 chord in any key
to have either a Major or a Seventh Chord Quality.* The choice is yours. But how
do you decide which to use? Compare **D** and **D7** in this chord progression:

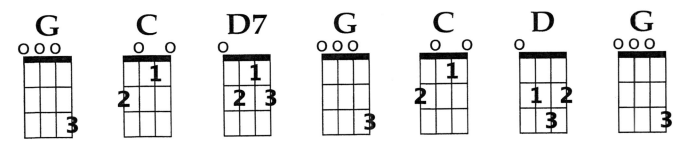

Do you hear the difference?

Major chords have a *consonant, pure, happy* sound.
Seventh chords sound slightly ***dissonant, edgy and restless***.

I only taught you the **D7** first because it's easier to play and you've got the 1st finger acting as an Anchor Finger during the change from **C**.

There are *quintillions* of folk, rock, blues and country songs that contain only the **1 - 4 - 5** chords. In any given key, the **1 chord** is the strongest, most magnetic of the three: first, last, most. The **4 chord** turns out to be a *friendly* sort of chord with regard to the **1 chord**; the two enjoy a relaxed interchange that could go on all day. Try alternating between **G** and **C**. Nice and easy.

But the **5 chord,** especially when it has the Seventh Chord Quality, is edgy, *pushy,* and wants to return, or **resolve**, to the **1 chord**. Mind you, the **5 chord** doesn't *need* to be a Seventh chord to experience this pull to the **1 chord**: The Major **5 chord** will also want to resolve there, it's just more compelling with the dissonant, unstable Seventh. Go back and play that last chord progression again to hear this.

We turn now to the 2nd, 3rd and 6th slots in the Chord Family Line-Up. These are the Minor chords, having a **Minor Chord Quality**. So in the **Key of G**, the **2 minor chord** is **Am,** the **3 minor chord** is **Bm** and the **6 minor chord** is **Em**.

Minor chords have a ***consonant, pure, sad, somber, blue, melancholy*** sound.
Of the three, the **6m** (here **Em**) is the most prevalent, and has the distinction of being named the **Relative Minor**. The **2m** is less common and the **3m** is downright scarce.

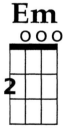 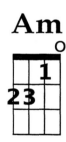 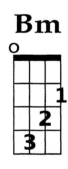

Em is so simple to finger I won't insult you by telling you. Of course, in the time it took me to tell you that, I could have just told you.

For **Am**, start with a **C** chord and tuck the 3rd finger in behind the 2nd. **Bm** is a diagonal chord occupying 4 frets; not difficult, but you must start it at the *2nd* fret of the 1st string.

Yes, Elizabeth, there is one more slot in the Chord Family, lucky number Seven. Now, don't mix this up with our other use of the number Seven, as in the "Seventh Chord Quality." This is like the difference between apples and orangutans.

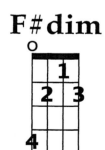

The **7 chord** has a **Diminished Chord Quality** and can be ignored for now. In the **G Chord Family**, the **7 chord** is the **F#dim** chord; similar to **D7**. (That "F" in the Alphabet on the previous page is really an "F#"; I'll explain later.) Anyway, here's the new chord. Enjoy!

Songs in the Key of G

I won't be throwing *too* many songs at you, for several reasons. One, there are plenty of songbooks and Web sites available to help you learn to play song after song. Two, copyright law forbids me from using any song that is younger than 70 years old. No "Margaritaville," no "Maxwell's Silver Hammer." I'd rather get you to where you can figure out some of this stuff on your own. You know, teach a man to fish and all.

In this first part of the book, I want you to learn mainly about the chords that belong to *5 Chord Families*: G, C, D, A and E. We call them, for some reason, the *C-A-G-E-D* Chord Families. So let's look at a smaller number of songs that *everyone* knows and that have typical and interesting chord progressions that demonstrate the most useful elements of music theory for the bari-uke.

We'll start off with songs that have chords that come from right out of the **G Chord Family**, then branch out from there to some "other" chords, ones that don't belong to the nuclear family as such, but can be regarded as cousins & uncles & sisters-in-law. Again, I'd rather put off the *riveting* explanations for all this until you've had a chance to get comfortable with making the chord changes and have some fun.

Before getting going, we have several "issues" to consider:

Issue #1: *What Note to Start Singing On.*

It turns out that for any given song, there are at least 3 different notes that you could start singing on, and while some people have an experienced enough ear to intuit the Starting Note and just jump right in, others do not. So what I shall do is to give you a Fretboard Diagram that displays an "S" on the Starting Note. If it's on an open string, I'll put the "S" right above that string. Might even give you *two positions* for the same note an octave apart, so that guys can go for the lower one, gals for the upper. ***Play the Starting Note by itself and try to match it with your voice.***

Issue #2: *How to Line Up the Words with the Chords.*

Again, some people just do this naturally and others could use a little help here. Right now, I'll lay out the measures with the "1 + 2 + 3 + 4 +" and situate the lyrics right over the specific counts where they are supposed to be sung. Once you know your way around each song, I'll start doing some abbreviating in the layout.

14

Let's start out with the chorus to a folk song that uses the **1 - 4 - 5 chords** in sequence, *La Bamba*. In fact, the chord sequence below is the sequence for *the entire song*. Sheesh. Try it first with the **D** chord as the **5 chord**, then compare it to the **D7** chord as the **5 chord**. Remember, the reason I'm bothering to discuss this **1 - 4 - 5** stuff is that, when we move to other keys, *the chords will be different, **but the numbers will remain the same***. Just use the **Down-Up** strum pattern we talked about before; the Starting Note (if you need it) and Fretboard Diagrams are at the bottom of the page.

G C	D	G C	D7
Bam - ba	Bamba	Bam - ba	Bamba

1 + 2 + 3 + 4 +   1 + 2 + 3 + 4 +   1 + 2 + 3 + 4 +   1 + 2 + 3 + 4 +

Here's **Jingle Bells**. Typical Hawaiian fare. Again, use Down-Ups and find the Starting Note and (the same) chords below. The scale is larger so I can fit in all the words. Either **D7** or **D**.

G

Jingle bells, jingle bells	jingle all the way

1   +   2   +   3   +   4   +   1   +   2   +   3   +   4   +

C   G

Oh, what fun it is to ride in a	one-horse open sleigh

1   +   2   +   3   +   4   +   1   +   2   +   3   +   4   +

G

Jingle bells, jingle bells	jingle all the way

1   +   2   +   3   +   4   +   1   +   2   +   3   +   4   +

C   G

Oh, what fun it is to ride in a	one horse open sleigh

1   +   2   +   3   +   4   +   1   +   2   +   3   +   4   +

open 3rd string **S** — **$** — *Bam -*

open 2nd string **S** — *Jingle...*

G   **C**   **D**   **D7**

Let's move on to *You Are My Sunshine*. Try the Country Strum Pattern. There are three words that precede that first measure: "**You are my**......"

G									G							
sun	-	shine,			my	only			sun	-	shine,			you	make me
1	+	2	+	3	+	4	+		1	+	2	+	3	+	4	+

C									G							
hap	-	py			when	skies	are		gray,					you'll	never
1	+	2	+	3	+	4	+		1	+	2	+	3	+	4	+

C									G							
know,		dear,			how	much	I		love		you,			please	don't
1	+	2	+	3	+	4	+		1	+	2	+	3	+	4	+

G		D7							G							
take		my	sun	-	shine	a	-		way						
1	+	2	+	3	+	4	+		1	+	2	+	3	+	4	+

Next comes *Auld Lang Syne*. Same Starting Note as above, and try the Rock Strum. There is one word that precedes that first measure: "**Should**...."

G									D7							
auld		ac	-	quain	-	tance			be		for	-	got		and
1	+	2	+	3	+	4	+		1	+	2	+	3	+	4	+

G									C							
never			brought		to				mind,						should
1	+	2	+	3	+	4	+		1	+	2	+	3	+	4	+

G									D7							
auld		ac	-	quain	-	tance			be		for	-	got		and
1	+	2	+	3	+	4	+		1	+	2	+	3	+	4	+

C		D7							G							
days		of	auld		lang				syne						
1	+	2	+	3	+	4	+		1	+	2	+	3	+	4	+

16

Amazing Grace has the same Starting Note as the above two. Try the 3/4 Waltz Strum:

G			C		G	
A - maz - ing	grace, how	sweet the	sound that

1 + 2 + 3 +   1 + 2 + 3 +   1 + 2 + 3 +   1 + 2 + 3 +

G			D7			
saved a	wretch like	me,	I

1 + 2 + 3 +   1 + 2 + 3 +   1 + 2 + 3 +   1 + 2 + 3 +

G			C		G	
once was	lost, but	now I'm	found, was

1 + 2 + 3 +   1 + 2 + 3 +   1 + 2 + 3 +   1 + 2 + 3 +

G		D7		G		
blind, but	now I	see	

1 + 2 + 3 +   1 + 2 + 3 +   1 + 2 + 3 +   1 + 2 + 3 +

Okay, folks, time to *embrace the cliché*. Same Starting Note as ***Jingle Bells***. Folk Strum:

G			D7		
Tip - toe to the	win - dow, by the

1 + 2 + 3 + 4 +   1 + 2 + 3 + 4 +

G			C		
win - dow, that is	where I'll be, come

1 + 2 + 3 + 4 +   1 + 2 + 3 + 4 +

G			D7		
tip - toe through the	tu - lips with

1 + 2 + 3 + 4 +   1 + 2 + 3 + 4 +

G		D7	
me	Oooohhhhhhhhhhhhhh!

1 + 2 + 3 + 4 +   1 + 2 + 3 + 4 +

Beyond the 1 - 4 - 5 Chords

Now that you've had some face time with the Major **1 - 4 - 5 chords** in the **Key of G**, let's see some of the Minor chords in action, as well as some of those "other" chords that don't really belong to the nuclear family. Some are in-laws. Some are *outlaws*.

As to the Minor chords, you'll see only the **6m** and the **2m chords** in these songs. As I alluded to before, the **3m chord** is actually rather rarely played compared to the others, so you'll be playing **Em** and **Am** but not **Bm**. We'll see the **3m** later.

I also want to introduce a more abbreviated presentation for the song lyrics. I expect by now, at least for the songs we've used as examples so far, that you have a sense of where the lyrics should come with regard to the chord changes.

So I'm going to omit the numbering of the beats (1+2+3+4+) and simply present the lyrics with the chord symbols placed over the exact word where the chord change occurs. In addition, *I'll place the number of beats for which you need to play some chord as an exponent to that chord.*

So, *La Bamba* goes from looking like this.....

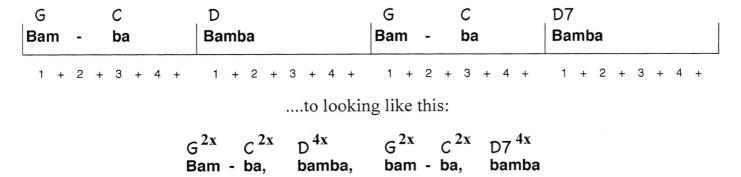

....to looking like this:

G^{2x} C^{2x} D^{4x} G^{2x} C^{2x} $D7^{4x}$
Bam - ba,   bamba,   bam - ba,   bamba

You know, save some trees. So here's *Jingle Bells* with the addition of a first cousin, **A7**:

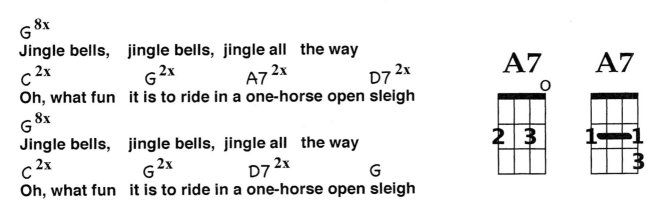

You could have used the 1st and 2nd fingers on that first **A7** shape instead of the 2nd and 3rd, but then *you would have missed the opportunity to move the 2nd and 3rd fingers as a unit into the D7 chord*. Kinda cool when you can do things like that, *and you should always be looking to do things like that*.

As for the second **A7** shape, this is a **barre chord**, where the 1st finger presses down all 4 strings and the 3rd finger adds one more note on top of the barre. Why the 3rd finger instead of the 2nd or 4th? *Because the 3rd finger is already holding down that note in the G chord and acts as an Anchor Finger.* Just add the barre below it. Then when you go on to the **D7**, the 3rd finger acts as a *Guide Finger*, sliding one fret down the same string.

Which **A7** shape is better? Dunno. The barre chord is harder, but the changes are very efficient, you must agree. Which one sounds better? That's up to you. Matter of taste.

The modified *Sunshine* also has two changes. The **G7** chord eats half of the **G** chord's lunch two separate times, and **Em** does it once. Slurp.

At least **Em** belongs to the **Key of G**, while **G7** technically does not. More on that later.

G ^{4x} G7 ^{4x}
You are my sunshine, my only sunshine
    C ^{4x} G ^{2x} G7 ^{2x}
You make me happy when skies are gray
    C ^{4x} G ^{2x} Em ^{2x}
You'll never know, dear, how much I love you
    G ^{2x} D7 ^{2x} G
Please don't take my sunshine a-way

The modified *Auld Lang Syne* has both **Em** and **G7**, and adds the **Am** chord, another member of the **G Chord Family**.

From **Em** to **Am**, you keep the 2nd finger as an Anchor, and from **Am** to **D7**, you keep the 1st finger as an Anchor.

   G ^{2x} Em ^{2x} Am ^{2x} D7 ^{2x}
Should auld ac-quaintance be for-got
   G ^{2x} G7 ^{2x} C ^{4x}
And never brought to mind
   G ^{2x} Em ^{2x} Am ^{2x} D7 ^{2x}
Should auld ac-quaintance be for-got
   C ^{2x} D7 ^{2x} G
And days of auld lang syne

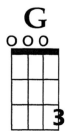 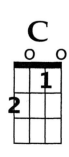 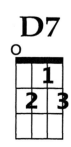 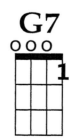 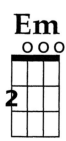 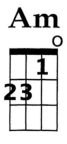 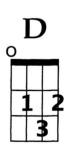

In the modified **Amazing Grace**, we again see a **G7**, an **Em** and an **Am**. Don't forget to try slipping in a plain old **D** chord instead of the **D7**. It's a purer sound, and some people prefer it, especially in a rock context.

Great Caesar's Ghost! What in the world is a **Cm6**? Just another dang barre chord. *Tiptoe* starts off tamely enough, then BAM! Too bad there's no help in the switch from **C** in the fingering, but it sounds great, in spite of Tiny Tim.

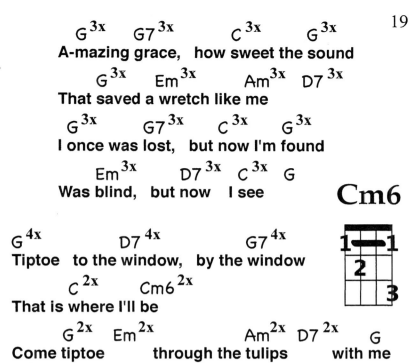

The Minor Sixth Chord Quality is not quite as sad as a pure Minor chord; more expectant. Turns out that **Cm6** is easier to play than the **Cm** in the same locale on the neck. But you don't *need* to change chords there at all; just play the C for 4x. If you do play the **Cm6**, you might consider using the **4th** finger instead of the 3rd if the stretch is too much; either way, you would keep that finger as an Anchor into the **G** chord that follows.

Now for a song that reaches way outside the **G Chord Family**: *Five Foot Two*.

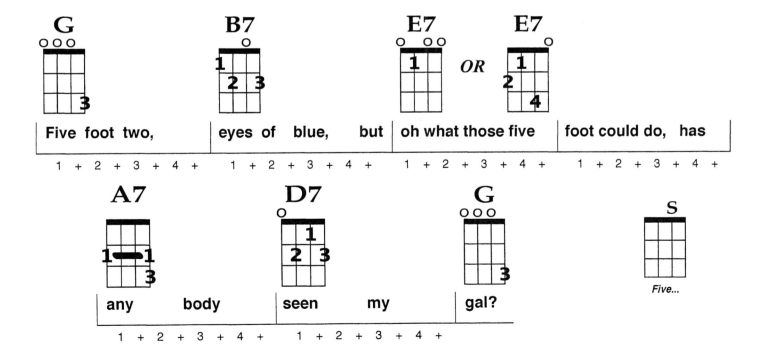

B7 and **E7** are the newbies here. From the opening **G** chord, you can Guide the 3rd finger down to the 2nd fret for **B7**. The first shape for **E7** is ridiculously easy to finger, but the second shape sounds better to me. I put the 4th finger in there instead of the 3rd to reduce the stretch, but either way is fine.

Here comes *Ain't She Sweet,* and now you're seeing the 4th finger all over the place:

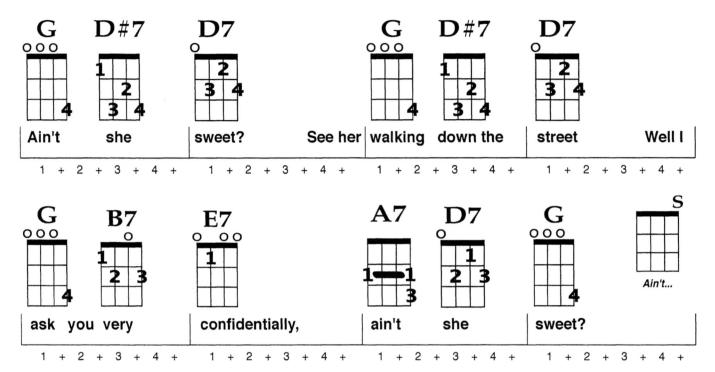

What's up with all those pinkies? I know the 4th finger is sort of a foppish dandy that mostly just lounges around, blinking and yawning, while others do the work, but it needn't be this way. In the present case, if you start with the 4th finger in the **G** instead of the 3rd, you get to keep it as an Anchor when you hit that second chord, the **D#7** (don't ask), and lay the 3 other fingers into position. Then you can Guide the whole chord down one fret to **D7** and then Guide the 4th finger back up to **G**. (**D#7** is one of those outlaws.)

This is much more efficient than sticking with the 3rd finger, and look at it this way: *You are training the 4th finger to show a little backbone and be useful, for Pete's sake!* You could continue to minimize its use, but you might as well have the whole team out on the court, even the wieners, because they *do* become stronger with use.

Change of subject. I want you to take notice of a particular sequence of *letters* in the chord names in the last two songs: ***B - E - A - D***. I'll have more to say about this later when I talk about the Great and Powerful **Circle of Fifths** in an upcoming section.

The C Chord Family

Time to change gears and become acquainted with the **Key of C**.
We'll do that by taking all the songs we just learned in the **Key of G**
and **transposing** them into the structure of the **C Chord Family**.
This is where all that **1 - 4 - 5** stuff will come into play.

Again, lay out the 7 letters of the Musical Alphabet, **ABCDEFG**, in order,
but starting with the Key Note, which in this case is **C**. Number them from 1 to 7.

C	D	E	F	G	A	B
1	2	3	4	5	6	7

Next, pick off the **1st**, **4th** and **5th** letters, which *this time* are **C, F** and **G**.

So the **1 chord**, the **4 chord** and the **5 chord**, which are the Major chords
in *any Chord Family Line-Up,* are **C, F** and **G** in the **Key of C**. Interesting that
the C and G chords were also in the **G Chord Family**, only THERE, the G
was the **1 chord** and the C was the **4 chord**. So now the C chord is the
home chord, the new F chord is the *friendly* chord and the old G chord
is the *push* chord, made even *pushier* as a Seventh chord, **G7**.

The Minor chords, the **2m, 3m** and **6m** chords, are **Dm, Em** and **Am**.
The **Am (6m)** is the Relative Minor, followed by the **Dm (2m)** and **Em (3m)**.
Dm is the only new Minor chord, as we saw the other two in the **Key of G**.
And this time, the **7 chord** is the **B Diminished**, or **Bdim**.

So let's take a look at these new chords.

The F chord is one of the trickiest of the basic chords.
You have to lay your 1st finger down *flat* over the 1st and
2nd strings, and then *arch* your 2nd and 3rd fingers in their
diagonal positions so that you don't deaden any strings.
The 1st finger is doing what is called a **partial barre**.

Dm is also a bit fingery, but not so bad. Of course,
you could use the 4th finger instead of the 3rd finger,
depending on where you're coming from or going to.

As for the **Bdim** chord, here, knock yourself out.

Songs in the Key of C

If you are struggling with the **F** chord, I hereby grant you permission *to cheat* by forgoing the partial barre and simply arching the 1st finger on the 2nd string. Then you can either deaden the 1st string or let it ring open.

The other new chord on this page, **C7**, is easy to make, and does not belong to the **Key of C**. (Seems odd that **C7** doesn't belong to the **Key of C**. If it's any consolation, neither do **Cm** or **Cm6**.)

Simpler

C 2x   F 2x   G 4x   C 2x   F 2x   G7 4x
Bam - ba,   Bamba,   Bam - ba,   Bamba

Bam -

C 8x
Jingle bells,   jingle bells, jingle all   the way
F 2x   C 2x   D7 2X   G7 2x
Oh, what fun   it is to ride in a one-horse open sleigh
C 8x
Jingle bells,   jingle bells, jingle all   the way
F 2x   C 2x   G7 2x   C
Oh, what fun   it is to ride in a one-horse open sleigh

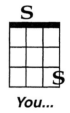
Jingle...

         C 4x   C7 4x
You are my sunshine, my only sunshine
           F 4x   C 2x   C7 2x
You make me happy when skies are gray
           F 4x   C 2x   Am 2x
You'll never know, dear, how much I love you
         C 2x   G7 2x   C
Please don't take my sunshine a-way

You...

C	F	G	G7	D7	C7	Am
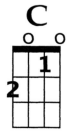	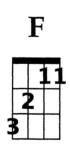	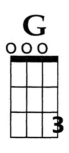	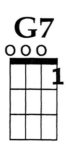	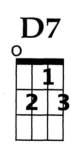	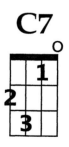	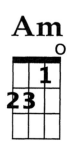

Here's your first chance to play the **Dm** chord.

C ^{2x} Am ^{2x} Dm ^{2x} G7 ^{2x}
Should auld ac-quaintance be   for-got
C ^{2x} C7 ^{2x} F ^{4x}
And never brought to mind
C ^{2x} Am ^{2x} Dm ^{2x} G7 ^{2x}
Should auld ac-quaintance be   for-got
F ^{2x} G7 ^{2x} C
And days of auld lang syne

C ^{3x} C7 ^{3x} F ^{3x} C ^{3x}
A-mazing grace, how sweet the sound
C ^{3x} Am ^{3x} Dm ^{3x} G7 ^{3x}
That saved a wretch like me
C ^{3x} C7 ^{3x} F ^{3x} C ^{3x}
I once was lost, but now I'm found
Am ^{3x} G7 ^{3x} F ^{3x} C
Was blind, but now   I see

Next, recall that back in *Tiptoe* in the **Key of G** we had the **Cm6** chord.
The analogous chord in the **Key of C** is **Fm6**, a partial barre at the 1st fret:

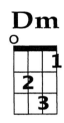

C ^{4x} G7 ^{4x} C7 ^{4x} F ^{2x} Fm6 ^{2x}
Tiptoe to the window, by the window, that is where I'll be
C ^{2x} Am ^{2x} Dm ^{2x} G7 ^{2x} C
Come tiptoe   through the tulips   with me

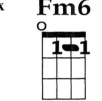

Below, when moving from **C** to **E7**, keep the 2nd finger as an Anchor Finger.
Another new chord is **G#7**, which is just the barre **A7** chord moved to the 1st fret.

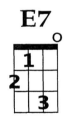

C ^{4x} E7 ^{4x} A7 ^{4x}
Five foot two, eyes of blue, but oh what those five foot could do
D7 ^{4x} G7 ^{4x} C
Has anybody   seen my   gal?

C ^{2x} G#7 ^{2x} G7 ^{4x} C ^{2x} G#7 ^{2x} G7 ^{4x}
Ain't   she   sweet? See her walking   down the street
C ^{2x} E7 ^{2x} A7 ^{4x} D7 ^{2x} G7 ^{2x} C
Well, I ask you very   confidentially, ain't   she   sweet?

 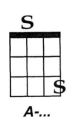 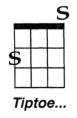 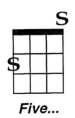 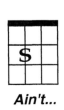

Should...   *A-...*   *Tiptoe...*   *Five...*   *Ain't...*

The D Chord Family

Let's move on, this time to the **Key of D**. Again, all of that "**1 - 4 - 5** Major" and "**2 - 3 - 6** Minor" jazz will be brought forward and shoehorned into a new key. Many of the chords will be familiar, since, as you know, Chord Families overlap.

Again, lay out the 7 letters of the Musical Alphabet, **ABCDEFG**, in order, *but starting with the Key Note,* which in this case is **D**. Number them from 1 to 7. You'll soon see what's up with those sharp signs hanging off the F and the C.

D	E	F#	G	A	B	C#
1	2	3	4	5	6	7

Next, pick off the **1st**, **4th** and **5th** letters, which *this time* are **D**, **G** and **A**.

So the **1 chord**, the **4 chord** and the **5 chord**, which are the Major chords in the *Chord Family Line-Up,* are **D**, **G** and **A** in the **Key of D**. Now the **D** chord is the *home* chord, the **G** chord is the *friendly* chord and the **A** chord is the *push* chord, made even *pushier* as a Seventh chord, **A7**.

The Minor chords, the **2m**, **3m** and **6m** chords, are **Em**, **F#m** and **Bm**. **Bm** (the **6m**) is the Relative Minor, followed by the **Em** (2m) and **F#m** (3m). **F#m** is the only new Minor chord, since we saw the other two in the **Key of G**. And this time, the **7 chord** is the **C# Diminished**, or **C#dim**. Forget about it.

We've seen **Am** and **A7**; now here's plain old **A**. You might wonder about this fingering, with the 1st finger wedged in between the 2nd and 3rd, but it's actually better than running 3 fingers in birth order, since *when you switch to D (which you will, often), you get to keep the 1st finger as an Anchor and use the 3rd finger as a Guide into the D fingering.* Lovely. Of course, you can always do it 1-2-3 or 2-3-4 instead.

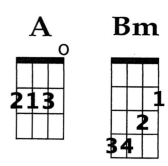

I prefer this 4-finger **Bm** chord over the 3-finger version I gave you before. This might be a tad harder, but sounds better. **F#m** is a barre chord, as well as the **3m**, so it won't show up much in the **Key of D**. I'll show it to you later.

Songs in the Key of D

Not much more to say about these boys.
Just jump on in there.

D ^{2x} G ^{2x} A ^{4x} D ^{2x} G ^{2x} A7 ^{4x}
Bam - ba,   Bamba,   Bam - ba,   Bamba

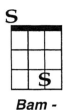
Bam -

D ^{8x}
Jingle bells, jingle bells, jingle all the way
G ^{2x} D ^{2x} E7 ^{2x} A7 ^{2x}
Oh, what fun it is to ride in a one-horse open sleigh
D ^{8x}
Jingle bells, jingle bells, jingle all the way
G ^{2x} D ^{2x} A7 ^{2x} D
Oh, what fun it is to ride in a one-horse open sleigh

Jingle...

       D ^{4x} D7 ^{4x}
You are my sunshine, my only sunshine
         G ^{4x} D ^{2x} D7 ^{2x}
You make me happy when skies are gray
         G ^{4x} D ^{2x} Bm ^{2x}
You'll never know, dear, how much I love you
       D ^{2x} A7 ^{2x} D
Please don't take my sunshine a-way

You...

D G A A7 A7 E7 D7 Bm

26

D²ˣ Bm²ˣ Em²ˣ A7²ˣ	D³ˣ D7³ˣ G³ˣ D³ˣ
Should auld ac-quaintance be for-got	A-mazing grace, how sweet the sound

D²ˣ D7²ˣ   G⁴ˣ
And never brought to mind

D³ˣ   Bm³ˣ   Em³ˣ   A7³ˣ
That saved a wretch like me

D²ˣ Bm²ˣ Em²ˣ A7²ˣ
Should auld ac-quaintance be for-got

D³ˣ   D7³ˣ   G³ˣ   D³ˣ
I once was lost, but now I'm found

G²ˣ A7²ˣ   D
And days of auld lang syne

Bm³ˣ   A7³ˣ   G³ˣ   D
Was blind, but now   I see

Another new chord from outside the family is **Gm**, and here are two fingerings. The non-barre version, on the left, makes better use of Anchor Fingers.

Gm

D⁴ˣ   A7⁴ˣ   D7⁴ˣ   G²ˣ   Gm²ˣ
Tiptoe to the window, by the window, that is where I'll be

D²ˣ   Bm²ˣ   Em²ˣ A7²ˣ   D
Come tiptoe   through the tulips   with me

Gm

F#7

As we did with the **Keys of G** and **C**, we'll reach even farther beyond the Chord Family with our final two examples. The **F#7** chord has a barre and a non-barre version; you pick. **A#7** is just an A7 chord that has been "sharped" (raised) by one fret.

D⁴ˣ   F#7⁴ˣ   B7⁴ˣ
Five foot two, eyes of blue, but oh what those five foot could do

B7

E7⁴ˣ   A7⁴ˣ   D
Has anybody seen my gal?

F#7

D²ˣ   A#7²ˣ A7⁴ˣ   D²ˣ   A#7²ˣ A7⁴ˣ
Ain't   she   sweet? See her walking   down the street

D²ˣ   F#7²ˣ   B7⁴ˣ   E7²ˣ A7²ˣ   D
Well, I ask you very   confidentially, ain't   she   sweet?

A#7

I must again point out the presence of the word "**BEAD**" as a sequence of letters in the names of chords in the last five songs, just like in the **Key of G**. Spooky, hmm?

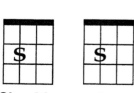 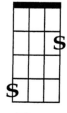 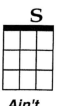

Should...   A-...   Tiptoe...   Five...   Ain't...

Patriotic Interlude

Have a go at *America, the Beautiful* in each of our three keys so far. I won't give you any Starting Notes, timings or handy Chord Diagrams this time; good luck, Young Uker.

I *will* tell you that the final melody note in one key is the same as the Starting Note in the next key. You just need to get the thing started in the **Key of D**.

Key of **D**

```
         D          A         Em   A7    D    A7
O beautiful for spacious skies, for amber waves of grain
         D          A7        A    E7    A7
For purple mountain majesties above the fruited plain
   D       G  A7    Em   A7   D    D7
America,   America, God shed his grace on thee
      G           D    Bm   Em   A7   D
And crown thy good with brotherhood from sea to shining sea
```

Key of **G**

```
  D7    G          D         Am   D7    G    D7
O beautiful for spacious skies, for amber waves of grain
         G          D7        D    A7    D7
For purple mountain majesties above the fruited plain
   G       C  D7    Am   D7   G    G7
America,   America, God shed his grace on thee
      C           G    Em   Am   D7   G
And crown thy good with brotherhood from sea to shining sea
```

Key of **C**

```
  G7    C          G         Dm   G7    C    G7
O beautiful for spacious skies, for amber waves of grain
         C          G7        G    D7    G7
For purple mountain majesties above the fruited plain
   C       F  G7    Dm   G7   C    C7
America,   America, God shed his grace on thee
      F           C    Am   Dm   G7   C
And crown thy good with brotherhood from sea to shining sea
```

The A Chord Family

The **Key of A** doesn't show up so often, but you should know something about it. Again, you'll see mostly chords that you've seen before---which is part of why this stuff can be confusing: Chord Families keep overlapping, and you really need to keep track of the **1 - 4 - 5**'s, at least, for the different keys. There's **G - C - D**. There's **C - F - G**. There's **D - G - A**. And now we'll figure out the situation for the **Key of A**.

Again, lay out the 7 letters of the Musical Alphabet, **ABCDEFG**, in order, *but starting with the Key Note,* which in this case is **A**. Number them from 1 to 7.

A	B	C#	D	E	F#	G#
1	2	3	4	5	6	7

Next, pick off the **1st**, **4th** and **5th** letters, which *this time* are **A**, **D** and **E**.

So the **1 chord**, the **4 chord** and the **5 chord**, which are the Major chords in the *Chord Family Line-Up*, are **A**, **D** and **E** in the **Key of A**. Now the **A** chord is the *home* chord, the **D** chord is the *friendly* chord and the **E** chord is the *push* chord, made even *pushier* as a Seventh chord, **E7**.

The Minor chords, the **2m**, **3m** and **6m chords**, are **Bm**, **C#m** and **F#m**. **F#m** (the **6m**) is the Relative Minor, followed by the **Bm** (**2m**) and **C#m** (**3m**). **C#m** is the only new Minor chord, and we won't bother with the **G# Diminished**. I don't think I'll even show you the **C#m** yet, since it's the rare **3m chord**.

Our Examples:

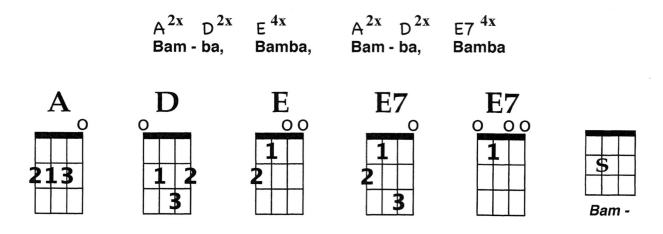

B7

A7

F#m

A ^{8x}
Jingle bells,   jingle bells,   jingle all   the way
D ^{2x} A ^{2x} B7 ^{2x} E7 ^{2x}
Oh, what fun   it is to ride in a one-horse open sleigh
A ^{8x}
Jingle bells,   Batman smells,   Robin laid an egg
D ^{2x} A ^{2x} E7 ^{2x} A
Batmobile   lost a wheel   and the Joker got a-way

A ^{4x} A7 ^{4x}
You are my sunshine, my only sunshine
D ^{4x} A ^{2x} A7 ^{2x}
You make me happy when skies are gray
D ^{4x} A ^{2x} F#m ^{2x}
You'll never know, dear, how much I love you
A ^{2x} E7 ^{2x} A
Please don't take my sunshine a-way

Nice Anchor Finger

A ^{2x} F#m ^{2x} Bm ^{2x} E7 ^{2x}
Should auld ac-quaintance be   for-got
A ^{2x} A7 ^{2x} D ^{4x}
And never brought to mind
A ^{2x} Bm ^{2x} E7 ^{2x}
Should auld ac-quaintance be   for-got
D ^{2x} E7 ^{2x} A
And days of auld lang syne

A ^{3x} A7 ^{3x} D ^{3x} A ^{3x}
A-mazing grace,   how sweet the sound
A ^{3x} F#m ^{3x} Bm ^{3x} E7 ^{3x}
That saved a wretch like me
A ^{3x} A7 ^{3x} D ^{3x} A ^{3x}
I once was lost,   but now I'm found
F#m ^{3x} E7 ^{3x} D ^{3x} A
Was blind,   but now   I see

Dm

A ^{4x} E7 ^{4x} A7 ^{4x} D ^{2x} Dm ^{2x}
Tiptoe   to the window,   by the window,   that is where I'll be
A ^{2x} F#m ^{2x} Bm ^{2x} E7 ^{2x} A
Come tiptoe   through the tulips   with me

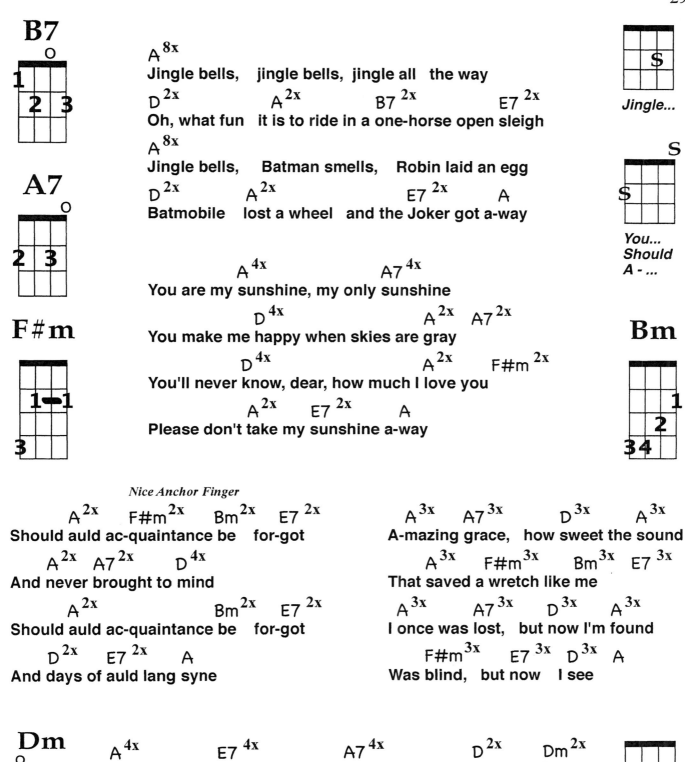

Jingle...

You...
Should
A - ...

Bm

Tiptoe...

The E Chord Family

The **Key of E** doesn't show up so often either, but probably more than the **Key of A**. Notice I didn't run you through *Five Foot Two* and *Ain't She Sweet* for the **Key of A**. Well, I won't do it for the **Key of E**, either. The some of chords needed for those songs are just too far afield for you to be worried about right now. So, on to the **Key of E**.

Again, lay out the 7 letters of the Musical Alphabet, **ABCDEFG**, in order, *but starting with the Key Note,* which in this case is **E**. Number them from 1 to 7.

E	F#	G#	A	B	C#	D#
1	2	3	4	5	6	7

Next, pick off the **1st, 4th** and **5th** letters, which *this time* are **E, A** and **B**.

So the **1 chord**, the **4 chord** and the **5 chord**, which are the Major chords in the *Chord Family Line-Up,* are **E, A** and **B** in the **Key of E**. The **E** chord is the *home* chord, the **A** chord is the *friendly* chord and the **B** chord is the *push* chord, made even *pushier* as a Seventh chord, **B7**.

Of course, we've been using **B7** since way back in the **Key of G**. But the plain old **B** chord is new, and it's not so bad, really (see below), but most people choose to play the **B7** chord instead of the **B** anyway. And try the two new sequential fingerings for **A**: The 2-3-4 works best on the way to **B**, and the 1-2-3 works best on the way to **B7**.

The Minor chords, the **2m, 3m** and **6m** chords, are **F#m, G#m** and **C#m**. **C#m** (the **6m**) is the Relative Minor, followed by the **F#m (2m)** and **G#m (3m)**. Since **G#m** is the elusive **3m chord** and **D#** is the weird **Diminished**, I won't be showing you either one. But I will show you **C#m** (it's easy peasy).

On to the examples:

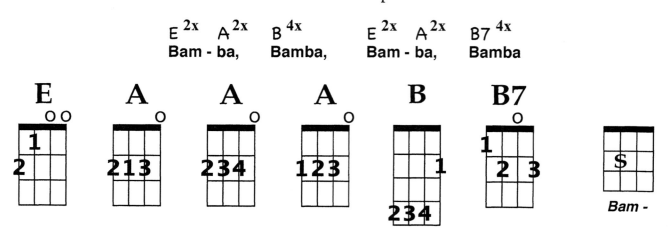

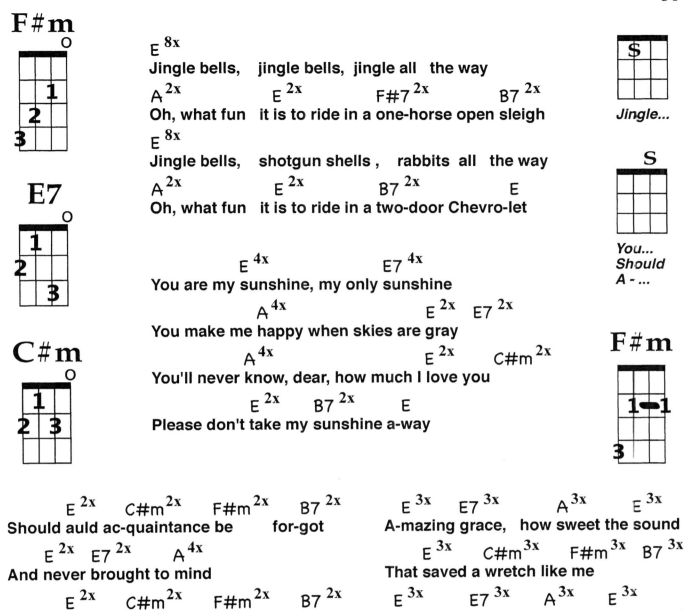

E ^{8x}
Jingle bells, jingle bells, jingle all the way
A ^{2x} E ^{2x} F#7 ^{2x} B7 ^{2x}
Oh, what fun it is to ride in a one-horse open sleigh
E ^{8x}
Jingle bells, shotgun shells , rabbits all   the way
A ^{2x} E ^{2x} B7 ^{2x} E
Oh, what fun it is to ride in a two-door Chevro-let

E ^{4x} E7 ^{4x}
You are my sunshine, my only sunshine
         A ^{4x} E ^{2x} E7 ^{2x}
You make me happy when skies are gray
         A ^{4x} E ^{2x} C#m ^{2x}
You'll never know, dear, how much I love you
         E ^{2x} B7 ^{2x} E
Please don't take my sunshine a-way

E ^{2x} C#m ^{2x} F#m ^{2x} B7 ^{2x}
Should auld ac-quaintance be   for-got
E ^{2x} E7 ^{2x} A ^{4x}
And never brought to mind
E ^{2x} C#m ^{2x} F#m ^{2x} B7 ^{2x}
Should auld ac-quaintance be   for-got
A ^{2x} B7 ^{2x} E
And days of auld lang syne

E ^{3x} E7 ^{3x} A ^{3x} E ^{3x}
A-mazing grace, how sweet the sound
E ^{3x} C#m ^{3x} F#m ^{3x} B7 ^{3x}
That saved a wretch like me
E ^{3x} E7 ^{3x} A ^{3x} E ^{3x}
I once was lost, but now I'm found
         C#m ^{3x} B7 ^{3x} A ^{3x} E
Was blind, but now   I see

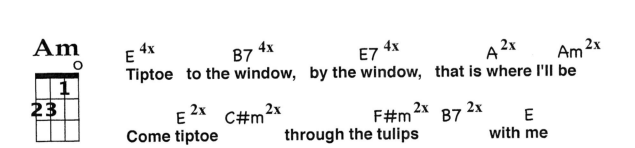

E ^{4x} B7 ^{4x} E7 ^{4x} A ^{2x} Am ^{2x}
Tiptoe to the window, by the window, that is where I'll be
      E ^{2x} C#m ^{2x} F#m ^{2x} B7 ^{2x} E
Come tiptoe   through the tulips   with me

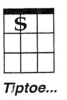

Tiptoe...

Quiz Time for the Chord Families

Here's a new batch of songs with *just the Chord Family numbers provided*. Pick a key, and then it's just like algebra, only fun: I give you the number and you plug in the corresponding letter/chord. You'll find a summary of the Chord Families on the next page. So for the **Key of G**, the **1 chord** is **G**, the **4 chord** is **C**, ad nauseum infinitum. Some of the chords may sound a bit "wrong" because I've taken some liberties for the sake of simplicity. We'll fix those problems later. You're on your own in terms of Starting Notes and pacing out the lyrics.

Complete this exercise to enter a state of unmitigated bliss and self-satisfaction.

1^{6x} 4^{6x}
Oh, give me a home where the buffalo roam

1^{6x} 5^{6x}
Where the deer and the antelope play

1^{6x} 4^{6x}
Where seldom is heard a dis-couraging word

1^{3x} 5^{3x} 1
And the skies are not cloudy all day

1^{3x} 4^{3x} 1^{6x}
My bonnie lies over the ocean

1^{3x} $6m^{3x}$ $2m^{3x}$ 5^{3x}
My bonnie lies over the sea

1^{3x} 4^{3x} 1^{6x}
My bonnie lies over the ocean

4^{3x} 5^{3x} 1
Oh, bring back my bonnie to me

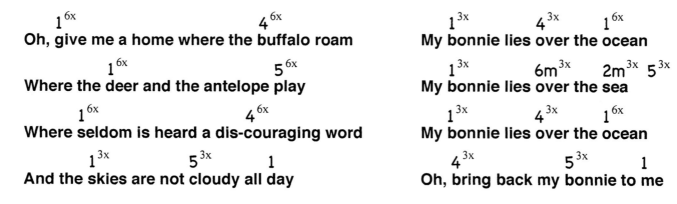

1^{3x} $2m^{3x}$ 5^{3x} 4^{3x} 1^{3x}
Morning has bro - ken,   like the first morn - ing

1^{3x} $3m^{3x}$ $6m^{3x}$ $2m^{3x}$ 5^{6x}
Blackbird has spok - en,   like the first bird

1^{3x} 4^{6x} 1^{3x} $6m^{3x}$ $2m^{3x}$
Praise for the singing, praise for the morn - ing

5^{3x} 1^{3x} 4^{3x} 5^{3x} 1
Praise for them spring - ing,   fresh from the world

1^{3x} 4^{1x} 1^{3x} 4^{1x} 1^{3x} 4^{1x} 1^{3x} 4^{1x}
Hoist up the John B.'s   sails,   see how the main-sail   sets

1^{3x} 4^{1x} 1^{4x} 5^{8x}
Call the captain a - shore, let me go home

1^{8x} 4^{1x} $2m^{4x}$
Let me go home,   I wanna go home, yeah, yeah

1^{4x} 5^{8x} 1^{4x}
Well, I feel so broke up,   I wanna go home

Our Five Chord Families

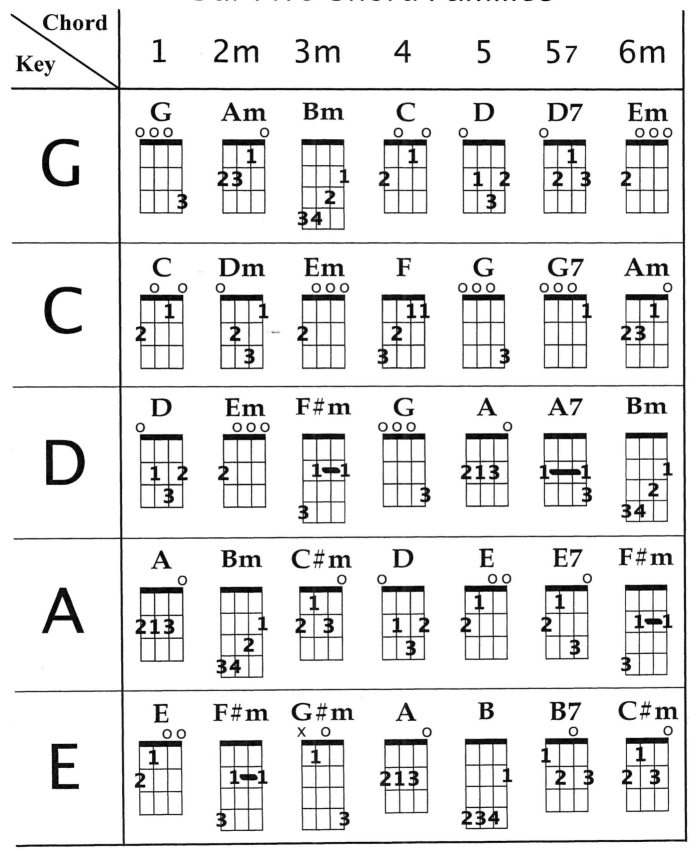

The F Chord Family, Just in Case

A song in the **Key of F** pops up once in a while; it's one of the flat keys, and I don't want to get into what that means right now, so let's just go on and identify which chords might find themselves under the province of the **F** chord.

Again, lay out the 7 letters of the Musical Alphabet, **ABCDEFG**, in order, *but starting with the Key Note*, which in this case is **F**. Number them from 1 to 7.

F	G	A	Bb	C	D	E
1	2	3	4	5	6	7

Next, pick off the **1st**, **4th** and **5th** letters, which *this time* are **F, Bb** and **C**.

So the **1 chord**, the **4 chord** and the **5 chord**, which are the Major chords in the *Chord Family Line-Up,* are **F, Bb** and **C** in the **Key of F**. The **F** chord is the *home* chord, the **Bb** chord is the *friendly* chord and the **C** chord is the *push* chord, made even *pushier* as a Seventh chord, **C7**.

The Minor chords, the **2m, 3m** and **6m chords**, are **Gm, Am** and **Dm**. **Dm** (the **6m**), the Relative Minor, is most prevalent, followed by the **Gm** (**2m**) and **Am** (**3m**). You've already seen the **Am** a lot and the **Dm** and **Gm** a little, so the only useful new chord in the **F Chord Family** is the **Bb** chord.

You already know the **B** chord, and you further know that "flat" means "lowered by one fret," so I think you can imagine what **Bb** looks like. But there is a 3-note version of the chord that I've listed next to the 4-note version, and the choice is entirely yours.

On to the examples:

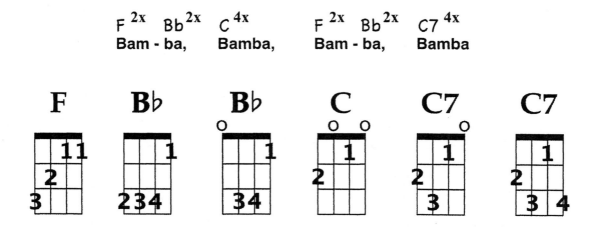

35

G7

Gm

F ⁸ˣ
Jingle bells,   Batman smells,   Robin laid an egg
Bb ²ˣ   F ²ˣ   G7 ²ˣ   C7 ²ˣ
Batmobile   lost a wheel and the Joker got a-way
F ⁸ˣ
Jingle bells,   shotgun shells,   rabbits all   the way
Bb ²ˣ   F ²ˣ   C7 ²ˣ   F
Oh, what fun   it is to ride in a two-door Chevro-let

Dm

Bbm

F ⁸ˣ
You are my sunshine, my only sunshine
           Bb ⁴ˣ   F ⁴ˣ
You make me happy when skies are gray
           Bb ⁴ˣ   F ²ˣ   Dm ²ˣ
You'll never know, dear, how much I love you
           F ²ˣ   C7 ²ˣ   F
Please don't take my sunshine a-way

F ²ˣ   Dm ²ˣ   Gm ²ˣ   C7 ²ˣ   F ⁶ˣ   Bb ³ˣ   F ³ˣ
Should auld ac-quaintance be   for-got   A-mazing grace,   how sweet the sound
F ⁴ˣ   Bb ⁴ˣ   F ³ˣ   Dm ²ˣ   Gm ²ˣ   C7 ²ˣ
And never brought to mind   That saved a wretch like me
F ²ˣ   Dm ²ˣ   Gm ²ˣ   C7 ²ˣ   F ⁶ˣ   Bb ³ˣ   F ³ˣ
Should auld ac-quaintance be   for-got   I once was lost,   but now I'm found
Bb ²ˣ   C7 ²ˣ   F   Dm ²ˣ   C7 ³ˣ   Bb ³ˣ   F
And days of auld lang syne   Was blind, but now   I see

     F ⁴ˣ   C7 ⁴ˣ   F ⁴ˣ   Bb ⁴ˣ   Bbm ⁴ˣ
Tiptoe   to the window,   by the window,   that is where I'll be
     F ²ˣ   Dm ²ˣ   Gm ²ˣ   C7 ²ˣ   F
Come tiptoe   through the tulips   with me

Full Arrangements in G and C

Here are full arrangements of some of our songs in the **Keys of G** and **C**. These are the two most popular keys on the bari-uke, and it turns out that they are "far enough away" from each other with regard to pitch that, if you are unable to manage the vocal range in one of them, you'll probably do fine in the other.

They start out simpler and then complexify as they go on, in order to build interest.

You Are My Sunshine

Key of G

G 8x
You are my sunshine, my only sunshine
 C 4x   G 4x
You make me happy when skies are gray
 C 4x   G 4x
You'll never know, dear, how much I love you
 G 2x   D7 2x   G 4x
Please don't take my sunshine a-way

 G 4x   G7 4x
The other night, dear, as I lay sleeping
 C 4x   G 4x
I dreamt I held you in my arms
 C 4x   G 2x Em 2x
When I a-wakened, I was mis-taken
 G 2x   D7 2x   G 4x
So I hung my head and I cried

 G 4x   G7 4x
You are my sunshine, my only sunshine
 C 4x   G 2x G7 2x
You make me happy when skies are gray
 C 4x   G 2x Em 2x
You'll never know, dear, how much I love you
 G 2x   D7 2x   G
Please don't take my sunshine a-way

Key of C

C 8x
You are my sunshine, my only sunshine
 F 4x   C 4x
You make me happy when skies are gray
 F 4x   C 4x
You'll never know, dear, how much I love you
 C 2x   G7 2x   C 4x
Please don't take my sunshine a-way

 G 4x   G7 4x
The other night, dear, as I lay sleeping
 C 4x   G 4x
I dreamt I held you in my arms
 C 4x   G 2x Em 2x
When I a-wakened, I was mis-taken
 G 2x   D7 2x   G
So I hung my head and I cried

 C 4x   C7 4x
You are my sunshine, my only sunshine
 F 4x   C 2x C7 2x
You make me happy when skies are gray
 F 4x   C 2x Am 2x
You'll never know, dear, how much I love you
 C 2x   G7 2x   C
Please don't take my sunshine a-way

Amazing Grace

Key of G

G^{6x} C^{3x} G^{3x}
A-mazing grace,   how sweet the sound
G^{6x} $D7^{6x}$
That saved a wretch like me
G^{6x} C^{3x} G^{3x}
I once was lost,   but now I'm found
G^{3x} $D7^{3x}$ G^{6x}
Was blind,   but now   I see

G^{6x} C^{3x} G^{3x}
'Twas grace that taught my heart to sing
G^{3x} Em^{3x} D^{3x} $D7^{3x}$
And grace my fears re-lieved
G^{3x} $G7^{3x}$ C^{3x} G^{3x}
How precious did that grace ap-pear
G^{3x} $D7^{3x}$ G^{6x}
The hour I first be-lieved

G^{3x} $G7^{3x}$ C^{3x} G^{3x}
Through many dangers, toils and snares
G^{3x} Em^{3x} Am^{3x} $D7^{3x}$
We have al-ready   come
G^{3x} $G7^{3x}$ C^{3x} G^{3x}
'Twas grace that brought us safe thus far
Em^{3x} $D7^{3x}$ C^{3x} G^{6x}
And grace will lead us home

G^{3x} $G7^{3x}$ C^{3x} G^{3x}
When we've been here ten thousand years
G^{3x} Em^{3x} Am^{3x} $D7^{3x}$
Bright shining as the   sun
G^{3x} $G7^{3x}$ C^{3x} G^{3x}
We've no less days to sing God's praise
Em^{3x} $D7^{3x}$ C^{3x} G
Than when we first be-gun

Key of C

C^{6x} F^{3x} C^{3x}
A-mazing grace,   how sweet the sound
C^{6x} $G7^{6x}$
That saved a wretch like me
C^{6x} F^{3x} C^{3x}
I once was lost,   but now I'm found
C^{3x} $G7^{3x}$ C^{6x}
Was blind,   but now   I see

C^{6x} F^{3x} C^{3x}
'Twas grace that taught my heart to sing
C^{3x} Am^{3x} G^{3x} $G7^{3x}$
And grace my fears re-lieved
C^{3x} $C7^{3x}$ F^{3x} C^{3x}
How precious did that grace ap-pear
C^{3x} $G7^{3x}$ C^{6x}
The hour I first be-lieved

C^{3x} $C7^{3x}$ F^{3x} C^{3x}
Through many dangers, toils and snares
C^{3x} Am^{3x} Dm^{3x} $G7^{3x}$
We have al-ready   come
C^{3x} $C7^{3x}$ F^{3x} C^{3x}
'Twas grace that brought us safe thus far
Am^{3x} $G7^{3x}$ F^{3x} C^{6x}
And grace will lead us home

C^{3x} $C7^{3x}$ F^{3x} C^{3x}
When we've been here ten thousand years
C^{3x} Am^{3x} Dm^{3x} $G7^{3x}$
Bright shining as the   sun
C^{3x} $C7^{3x}$ F^{3x} C^{3x}
We've no less days to sing God's praise
Am^{3x} $G7^{3x}$ F^{3x} C
Than when we first be-gun

Sloop John B.

Key of G

G⁸ˣ
We come on the Sloop John B.
G⁸ˣ
My grandfather and me
G⁸ˣ   D⁸ˣ
A-round Nassau Town we did roam
         G⁸ˣ   C⁸ˣ
Drinking all night,   got into a fight
     G⁴ˣ   D⁴ˣ   G⁸ˣ
Well, I feel so broke up,   I wanna go home

   G³ˣ   C¹ˣ G³ˣ   C¹ˣ
Hoist up the John B.'s sails
G³ˣ   C¹ˣ G³ˣ   C¹ˣ
See how the main-sail sets
G⁸ˣ   D⁴ˣ   D7⁴ˣ
Call the captain a - shore, let me go home
       G⁴ˣ   G7⁴ˣ   C⁴ˣ   Am⁴ˣ
Let me go home,   I wanna go home, yeah, yeah
     G⁴ˣ   D7⁴ˣ   G⁸ˣ
Well, I feel so broke up,   I wanna go home

       G³ˣ   C¹ˣ G³ˣ   C¹ˣ
The first mate, he got drunk
G³ˣ   C¹ˣ G³ˣ   C¹ˣ
Broke in the Cap-tain's trunk
   G⁸ˣ   D⁴ˣ   D7⁴ˣ
The constable had to come and take him a-way
      G⁴ˣ   G7⁴ˣ   C⁴ˣ   Am⁴ˣ
Sheriff John Stone,   why'd you leave me a-lone?
     G⁴ˣ   D7⁴ˣ   G⁸ˣ
Well, I feel so broke up,   I wanna go home

Repeat Chorus: "Hoist up..."

Key of C

C⁸ˣ
We come on the Sloop John B
C⁸ˣ
My grandfather and me
C⁸ˣ   G⁸ˣ
A-round Nassau Town we did roam
         C⁸ˣ   F⁸ˣ
Drinking all night,   got into a fight
     C⁴ˣ   G⁴ˣ   C⁸ˣ
Well, I feel so broke up,   I wanna go home

   C³ˣ   F¹ˣ C³ˣ   F¹ˣ
Hoist up the John B.'s sails
C³ˣ   F¹ˣ C³ˣ   F¹ˣ
See how the main-sail sets
C⁸ˣ   G⁴ˣ   G7⁴ˣ
Call the captain a - shore, let me go home
       C⁴ˣ   C7⁴ˣ   F⁴ˣ   Dm⁴ˣ
Let me go home,   I wanna go home, yeah, yeah
     C⁴ˣ   G7⁴ˣ   C⁸ˣ
Well, I feel so broke up,   I wanna go home

       C³ˣ   F¹ˣ C³ˣ   F¹ˣ
The first mate, he got drunk
C³ˣ   F¹ˣ C³ˣ   F¹ˣ
Broke in the Cap-tain's trunk
   C⁸ˣ   G⁴ˣ   G7⁴ˣ
The constable had to come and take him a-way
      C⁴ˣ   C7⁴ˣ   F⁴ˣ   Dm⁴ˣ
Sheriff John Stone,   why'd you leave me a-lone?
     C⁴ˣ   G7⁴ˣ   C⁸ˣ
Well, I feel so broke up,   I wanna go home

Repeat Chorus: "Hoist up..."

Morning Has Broken

There is an instrumental Interlude between the Verses as well as an Ending.

G³ˣ Am³ˣ D7³ˣ   C³ˣ   G³ˣ
Morning has bro - ken,   like the first morn - ing
G³ˣ   Bm³ˣ Em³ˣ A7³ˣ   D³ˣ D7³ˣ
Blackbird has spok - en,   like the first bird
G³ˣ   C⁶ˣ   G³ˣ   Em³ˣ A7³ˣ
Praise for the singing, praise for the morn - ing
D7³ˣ   G³ˣ   C³ˣ D7³ˣ   G³ˣ
Praise for them spring - ing,   fresh from the world

C³ˣ D7³ˣ B7³ˣ Em³ˣ C³ˣ   G³ˣ D7³ˣ   G

C³ˣ Dm³ˣ G7³ˣ   F³ˣ   C³ˣ
Morning has bro - ken,   like the first morn - ing
C³ˣ   Em³ˣ Am³ˣ D7³ˣ   G³ˣ G7³ˣ
Blackbird has spok - en,   like the first bird
C³ˣ   F⁶ˣ   C³ˣ   Am³ˣ D7³ˣ
Praise for the singing, praise for the morn - ing
G7³ˣ   C³ˣ   F³ˣ G7³ˣ   C³ˣ
Praise for them spring - ing,   fresh from the world

F³ˣ G7³ˣ E7³ˣ Am³ˣ F³ˣ   C³ˣ G7³ˣ   C

G³ˣ Am³ˣ D7³ˣ   C³ˣ   G³ˣ
Sweet the rain's new fall,   sunlit from heav - en
G³ˣ   Bm³ˣ Em³ˣ A7³ˣ   D³ˣ D7³ˣ
Like the first dew - fall   on the first grass
G³ˣ   C⁶ˣ   G³ˣ   Em³ˣ A7³ˣ
Praise for the sweetness of the fresh gar - den
D7³ˣ   G³ˣ C³ˣ D7³ˣ   G³ˣ
Sprung in com-plete-ness where His feet pass

C³ˣ D7³ˣ B7³ˣ Em³ˣ C³ˣ   G³ˣ D7³ˣ   G

C³ˣ Dm³ˣ G7³ˣ   F³ˣ   C³ˣ
Sweet the rain's new fall,   sunlit from heav - en
C³ˣ   Em³ˣ Am³ˣ D7³ˣ   G³ˣ G7³ˣ
Like the first dew - fall   on the first grass
C³ˣ   F⁶ˣ   C³ˣ   Am³ˣ D7³ˣ
Praise for the sweetness of the fresh gar - den
G7³ˣ   C³ˣ F³ˣ G7³ˣ   C²ˣ
Sprung in com-plete-ness where His feet pass

F³ˣ G7³ˣ E7³ˣ Am³ˣ F³ˣ   C³ˣ G7³ˣ   C

G³ˣ Am³ˣ D7³ˣ   C³ˣ   G³ˣ
Mine is the sun - light,   mine is the morn - ing
G³ˣ   Bm³ˣ Em³ˣ A7³ˣ   D³ˣ D7³ˣ
Born of the one   light Eden saw play
G³ˣ   C⁶ˣ   G³ˣ   Em³ˣ A7³ˣ
Praise with e-lation, praise every morn - ing
D7³ˣ   G³ˣ C³ˣ D7³ˣ   G³ˣ
God's recre - a - tion of the new day

C³ˣ G³ˣ C³ˣ G³ˣ C³ˣ G

C³ˣ Dm³ˣ G7³ˣ   F³ˣ   C³ˣ
Mine is the sun - light,   mine is the morn - ing
C³ˣ   Em³ˣ Am³ˣ D7³ˣ   G³ˣ G7³ˣ
Born of the one   light Eden saw play
C³ˣ   F⁶ˣ   C³ˣ   Am³ˣ D7³ˣ
Praise with e-lation, praise every morn - ing
G7³ˣ   C³ˣ F³ˣ G7³ˣ   C³ˣ
God's recre - a - tion of the new day

F³ˣ C³ˣ F³ˣ C³ˣ F³ˣ C

Five Foot Two

G ^{4x} B7 ^{4x}
Five foot two,   eyes of blue
     E7 ^{4x}
But oh what those five foot could do
     A7 ^{4x} D7 ^{4x} G ^{4x} D7 ^{4x}
Has anybody   seen my   gal?

G ^{4x} B7 ^{4x}
Turned up nose,   turned down hose
E7 ^{4x}
Never had no other beaus
     A7 ^{4x} D7 ^{4x} G ^{2x} C ^{2x} G ^{4x}
Has anybody   seen my   gal?

       B7 ^{8x}
Now if you run into a five-foot two
E7 ^{8x}
Covered with furs
A7 ^{8x}
Diamond rings and all those things
D7 ^{4x}
Bet your life it isn't her

G ^{4x} B7 ^{4x}
But could she love,   could she woo?
E7 ^{4x}
Could she,   could she, could she coo?
     A7 ^{4x} D7 ^{4x} G ^{2x} C ^{2x} G
Has anybody   seen my   gal?

C ^{4x} E7 ^{4x}
Five foot two,   eyes of blue
     A7 ^{4x}
But oh what those five foot could do
     D7 ^{4x} G7 ^{4x} C
Has anybody   seen my   gal?

C ^{4x} E7 ^{4x}
Turned up nose,   turned down hose
A7 ^{4x}
Never had no other beaus
     D7 ^{4x} G7 ^{4x} C ^{2x} F ^{2x} C ^{4x}
Has anybody   seen my   gal?

       E7 ^{8x}
Now if you run into a five-foot two
A7 ^{8x}
Covered with furs
D7 ^{8x}
Diamond rings and all those things
G7 ^{4x}
Bet your life it isn't her

C ^{4x} E7 ^{4x}
But could she love,   could she woo?
A7 ^{4x}
Could she,   could she, could she coo?
     D7 ^{4x} G7 ^{4x} C ^{2x} F ^{2x} C
Has anybody   seen my   gal?

The *Circle of Fifths* or 'BEAD'GC or
Bruce Emery Ate Dandelion Greens and Cauliflowers

Several times now, I have pointed out a specific sequence of chords:
B-E-A-D. This is one segment of a musical tool called the **Circle of Fifths**.

See, music, left to its own devices, likes to travel *backward by a 5th*.
Think back to the **Key of C**, where C was the **1 chord** and G was the **5 chord**,
(where you start counting from the letter C and go up 5 letters: C - D - E - F - G.)
We said that the **5 chord** wants to push back, or return, or **resolve**, to the **1 chord**.
It's called **Root Movement Downward by a 5th**, a compelling force in music.

*Well, this happens in all 12 keys, this 5 - 1 resolution, and it is so powerful
a force that it **cuts right across the borders between keys**.* Now bear with me:

These are individual 5 - 1 resolutions that overlap and link all the keys together:

In the **Key of C**, the **G** chord goes to the C chord: **G** to **C**.

In the **Key of G**, the **D** chord goes to the G chord: **D** to **G**.
*So if you **overlap** these keys, **D** goes to **G** goes to **C**.*

In the **Key of D**, the **A** chord goes to the **D** chord: **A** to **D**.
*So if you overlap ALL these keys, **A** goes to **D** goes to **G** goes to **C**.*

In the **Key of A**, the **E** chord goes to the **A** chord: **E** to **A**.
*So if you overlap these keys, **E** goes to **A** goes to **D** goes to **G** goes to **C**.*

In the **Key of E**, the **B** chord goes to the **E** chord: **B** to **E**.
*So if you overlap these keys, **B** goes to **E** goes to **A** goes to **D** goes to **G** goes to **C**.*

Proof that **Bruce Emery Ate Dandelion Greens and Cauliflowers**

It may be a little hard to swallow, because it seems
so simple, but this **Root Movement Downward by a 5th**
is what propels all of Western classical and popular music.
The full sequence includes all 12 keys, as illustrated in
the diagram, although we ukers care about only
the segment BEADGC, and sometimes F.

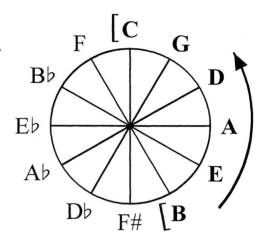

To read this thing for our *C-A-G-E-D* keys,
start with the **B** at the 5 o'clock position and read
backwards or *counter-clockwise* to land at **C**.
This is known as **backcycling** through the Circle,
and the chords can be Majors, Minors or Sevenths.

*(Conversely, you can read it **clockwise** from C, where each successive letter is UP a **5th**.
This will come in handy later.)*

. . . .

You are probably wondering, ***By cracky, what does all this have to do with me?***
Using the Circle of Fifths, I want to explain **Three Phenomena** that you've been
seeing in our little catalog of songs that go above and beyond the simple **1 - 4 - 5** stuff.
I'll use the **Key of G** for the examples, but any key would serve.

1st Phenomenon

G   G7   C   G
A-mazing grace, how sweet the sound

That **G7** right there. To all appearances, you are moving from a **1 chord** having a
Major Chord Quality to a **1 chord** with a Seventh Chord Quality, then on to the **4 chord**.
But no-o-o! The rule states that *only a **5 chord** in a Chord Family can be a Seventh chord*,
so this **G7** chord must be acting as a **5 chord** in another key, to wit, the **Key of C**, because
G goes to C (Greens to Cauliflowers), so we must now be, momentarily, in the **Key of C**.
And look! That's a **C** chord coming next, so we did a **5 - 1** progression in the **Key of C**.
A Lumper would say we never *really* left the **Key of G**, but a Splitter would say Uh-*HUH*!

Quiz: What's going on *here?* The **C7** chord
is the **5 chord** in the **Key of F** (see Circle),
so we are backcycling, temporarily, to
the **Key of F**. Then it's back to **C**.

C ^{3x} C7 ^{3x} F ^{3x} C ^{3x}
A-mazing grace, how sweet the sound

2nd Phenomenon

This next one even has an official name.....wait for it!.....*The Rhythm Changes!*
It refers to a chord progression you've seen before: **1 - 6m - 2m - 5**. Examples in **G**:

```
     G     Em      Am      D7   (G)
Should auld ac-quaintance be  for-got
```

```
     G    G7      C      G       G    Em     Am   D7  (G)
(A-mazing grace, how sweet the sound) That saved a wretch like me
```

```
       G    Em          Am   D7    G
Come tiptoe      through the tulips   with me
```

The monicker comes from the song *I Got Rhythm*, which uses this sequence.
Here's a bit of that one and some of the millions of others that use these 4 chords:

```
     G   Em  Am  D7     G    Em  Am  D7  (G)
 I   got rhy - thm,    I    got mus - ic
```

```
G    Em     Am  D7   (G)  |   G    Em  Am    D7       (G)
Take me out to the ball game |  Heart and soul  I fell in love with you
```

```
      G    Em  Am       D7       G   Em
Blue moon,        you saw me standing a-lone
Am          D7        G   Em  Am     D7      G
Without a dream in my heart,      without a love of my own
```

Look again at the Circle of Fifths. You start with **G** at the 1 o'clock position.
Then there's a *jump* clockwise to the **E** at 4 o'clock, then the backcycling
runs through **A** and **D**, finally settling down to the **G** again, at home.

Follow the backcycling in the Rhythm Changes in the **Keys of C** and **D**:

```
     C    Am     Dm    G7   (C)
Should auld ac-quaintance be  for-got
       Ate  Dandelion Greens & Cauliflowers

     D    Bm     Em    A7   (D)
Should auld ac-quaintance be  for-got
       Bruce  Emery  Ate  Dandelion = BEAD
```

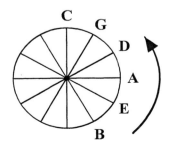

43

3rd Phenomenon

This one is just called *Secondary Dominants*. The **5 chord** in any key is also known as the **Dominant Chord**, since it's always trying to dominate the **1 chord**, or **Tonic Chord**. ("I am your father, Luke." "What we got here is a failure to communicate.")

Well, any of the chords that are clockwise from the **5 chord** in the Circle are called Secondary Dominants when they keep backcycling to the **1 chord**, *especially when they are Seventh chords,* but of course they can be Major or Minor chords instead.

And you can jump to any level and ride the wave back in. For example, in the **Key of G**, the **G** chord is the **1 chord** and the **D** chord is a **5th** above **G**. But the **A** chord, at 2 o'clock, is a **5th** above **D**, which is a **5th** above **G**, making the **A** chord the *5th of the 5th* of **G**. Here's an example:

G ^{8x}
Jingle bells,   jingle bells,   jingle all   the way

C ^{2x} G ^{2x} A7 ^{2x} D7 ^{2x}
Oh, what fun   it is to ride in a one-horse open sleigh

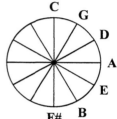

*(Check out **Morning Has Broken** for the same 5th of the 5th.)*

As I say, you can jump into the Secondary Dominants at any point clockwise from the **1 chord**. The example of ours that jumps the farthest is *Five Foot Two*. Here it is in three keys, and notice that *the overall BEADGC sequence doesn't change; we just use different segments from key to key*:

G ^{4x} B7 ^{4x} E7 ^{4x}
Five foot two, eyes of blue, but oh what those five foot could do

A7 ^{4x} D7 ^{4x} G
Has anybody seen my gal?   Here it's BEADG.

C ^{4x} E7 ^{4x} A7 ^{4x}
Five foot two, eyes of blue, but oh what those five foot could do

D7 ^{4x} G7 ^{4x} C
Has anybody seen my gal?   Here it's EADGC.

D ^{4x} F#7 ^{4x} B7 ^{4x}
Five foot two, eyes of blue, but oh what those five foot could do

E7 ^{4x} A7 ^{4x} D
Has anybody seen my gal?   Dawg! Here we need to jump all the way to F# (6 o'clock) on the Circle, giving us **F#BEAD**.

This is the
5th
of the
5th
of the
5th
of the
5th!

44

Yuletide Backcycling in G and C

45

You crave MORE EXAMPLES to be firmly convinced that everything I have said is the Truth, the whole Truth and nothing but the Truth except for the parts I made up. Christmas carols are full of Secondary Dominants as well as various other twists and turns. Let's jump to different levels in the Circle of Fifths and see what the ride down is like:

```
     G          D7     G     C      G   D
O come all ye faithful,  joyful and tri-um-phant
     Em       D       (A7)    D7
O come ye, o come ye to Be - eth-le-hem
     G          D7  G    D        A7    D7
Come and be-hold him, born the King of Angels
     G      C   G              C    G   D
O come let us a-dore him,  o come let us a-dore him
       C      A7  D7  C    G    D    G
O come let us a-dore him, Chri-ist the Lord
```

A7 is the **5th** of the **5th** of G

```
     G          D7   G              Am       D7   G
O Christmas tree, o  Christmas tree,  how beautiful and bright
D7  G           D7  G               Am       D7   G
O   Christmas tree, o  Christmas tree,  how beautiful and bright
     G          D7                 Am          D7   G
The sight of thee at Christmas tide spreads hope and glad-ness far and wide
D7  G           D7 (E7)            Am       D7   G
O   Christmas tree, o  Christmas tree,  how beautiful and bright
```

E7 is the **5th** of the **5th** of the **5th** of G

```
   G    C    G               C      A7    D7
It came up-on the midnight clear, that glorious song of old
   G    C    G               C       D7    G
From angels bending near the earth to touch their harps of gold
(B7)        Em              D       A7    D7
"Peace on the earth, good will to men, from heaven's all-gracious king"
   G    C    G          C      D7    G
The world in solemn stillness lay to hear the angels sing
```

B7 is the **5th** of the **5th** of the **5th** of the **5th** of G

```
   G           C       A7         D7
We wish you a Merry Christmas,  we wish you a Merry Christmas
(B7)       Em        A7    D7   G
We wish you a Merry Christmas and a Happy New Year
```

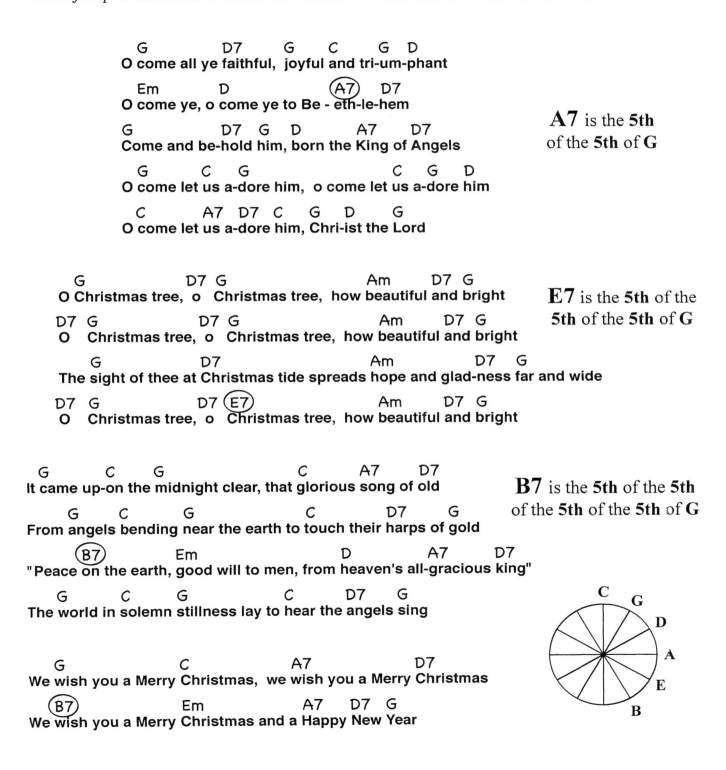

Notice that you don't always go straight down the chute,
but there's always a healthy push to do so. Here's the **Key of C**:

```
    C        G7     C    F    C   G
    O come all ye faithful,  joyful and tri-um-phant
      Am        G          (D7)   G7
    O come ye, o come ye to Be - eth-le-hem
    C           G7  C   G      D7    G7
    Come and be-hold him, born the King of Angels
      C      F    C            F    C    G
    O come let us a-dore him,  o come let us a-dore him
      F       D7 G7  F    C    G    C
    O come let us a-dore him, Chri-ist the Lord
```

D7 is the **5th**
of the **5th** of **C**

```
  C               G7  C           Dm        G7  C
  O Christmas tree, o  Christmas tree,  how beautiful and bright
G7  C            G7  C           Dm        G7  C
  O   Christmas tree, o  Christmas tree,  how beautiful and bright
     C            G7            Dm          G7   C
  The sight of thee at Christmas tide spreads hope and glad-ness far and wide
G7  C           G7 (A7)         Dm        G7  C
  O   Christmas tree, o  Christmas tree,  how beautiful and bright
```

A7 is the **5th** of the
5th of the **5th** of **C**

```
C      F    C           F    D7    G7
It came up-on the midnight clear, that glorious song of old
    C    F    C         F       G7    C
From angels bending near the earth to touch their harps of gold
  (E7)       Am            G      D7   G7
"Peace on the earth, good will to men, from heaven's all-gracious king"
  C    F    C        F    G7   C
The world in solemn stillness lay to hear the angels sing
```

E7 is the **5th** of the **5th**
of the **5th** of the **5th** of **C**

```
  C           F       D7        G7
We wish you a Merry Christmas,  we wish you a Merry Christmas
  E7          Am        D7 G7  C
We wish you a Merry Christmas and a Happy New Year
```

Fingerpicking: 1. Arpeggios in 4/4

We come to one of My Favorite Things to do: fingerstyle playing. This is where the fingers of the right hand activate the strings by plucking them, either 1, 2, 3 or 4 at a time, to produce a warmer, more intimate effect. By now, you can already strum and you have a lot of chording experience under your belt, so let's find a different musical "voice" for you to try, your "inside" voice, as it were.

Assume the position: Assign your **Thumb, Index, Middle** and **Ring** fingers to **4th, 3rd, 2nd** and **1st** strings respectively. Lay 'em down there. The Thumb will play *downward* and the 3 fingers will play *upward*. Squeeze the strings slightly and pluck them together (avoid pulling away), and try to get them all to ring with equal volume. Keep your hand *rotated* so that your Thumb moves past your fingers.

We're going to return to our **Tablature** notation, but now we're going to use *numbers* to indicate *which frets* of which *strings* you're supposed to play and at exactly what *time*.

The 4 lines represent the 4 strings of the ukulele. The top line corresponds to the 1st string, the one with the highest pitch. 2nd line, 2nd string. 3rd line, 3rd string. 4th line, 4th string.

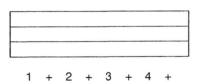

The numbers below the 4th line show the passage of **4/4 Time**, with the counts "One - & - Two - & - Three - & - Four - &."

The next diagram shows a **G** chord being played as an **arpeggio**. "Arpeggio" means "harp-like," with notes being played one at a time, here **ascending** in pitch.

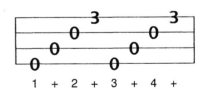

The first 3 notes are zeroes ("0"), which indicate open strings, and the "3" means 3rd fret. So here's what this Tab is telling you, as you hold down a **G** chord and map your fingers to the strings as I mentioned above (Thumb on 4, Index on 3, and so on):

On *Count 1*, play the open 4th string with the Thumb.
On *Count 1+*, play the open 3rd string with the Index finger.
On *Count 2*, play the open 2nd string with the Middle finger.
On *Count 2+*, play *fretted* 1st string (3rd fret) with the Ring Finger.
Then repeat for Counts 3 + 4 +.

Actually, without knowing in advance *what* chord I wanted you to play, you could figure out that it was a **G** chord from the **0-0-0-3** across the 4 strings. What if I gave you: **2-0-1-0**?
*4th string at 2nd fret...3rd string open...2nd string at 1st fret...1st string open...= **C** chord.*

Now, I DO intend to keep identifying the chords, with names or shapes;
I'm just saying that you could figure them out for yourself from the Tab.
Remember: *The Tab Diagram does not show you **finger** numbers,*
it shows you FRET numbers. *Fretboard Diagrams show fingers.*

Here's an exercise on the **G** chord. Keep your fingers moving continuously---don't pause before starting over with the Thumb (**Counts 1** and **3**). The pattern changes in Measure 3.

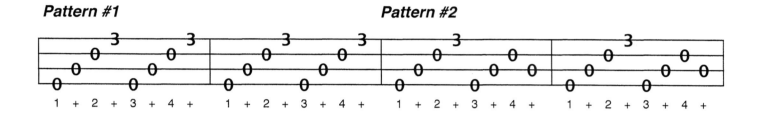

Pattern #1 is just a good default arpeggio pattern, while ***Pattern #2*** is a variation that gives the Ring Finger a rest. But try to get used to using the Ring finger; it's fairly floppy, and most folks just keep it locked in the attic, mumbling and wheezing, but given half a chance, an active Ring finger can really juice up the level of your fingerpicking.

Here's ***Auld Lang Syne*** using the standard **G**, **C** and **D7** chords you are familiar with. You can use either picking pattern with it, but I've written it out for ***Pattern #2***. "Should..."

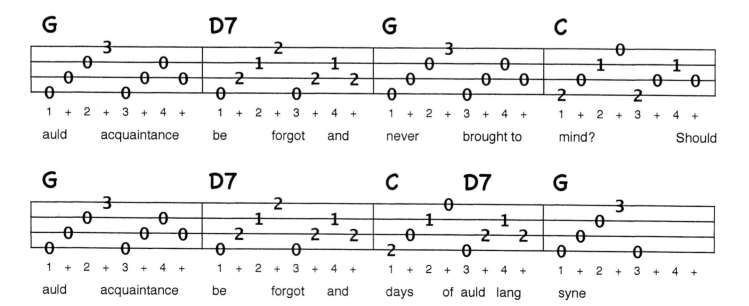

Here's the Chorus to *Sloop John B.*, and again, you can use either *Pattern #1* or *#2*. With a left-hand wrinkle! Look at Measures 1, 3 and 5 at **Count 4**: There's a "**1**" there (circled). So you'll add your 1st finger to the 2nd string at the 1st fret for just that beat, then remove it. If this bugs you, you can default to a plain **G** chord. And I'll be circling other non-standard notes that show up as we go.

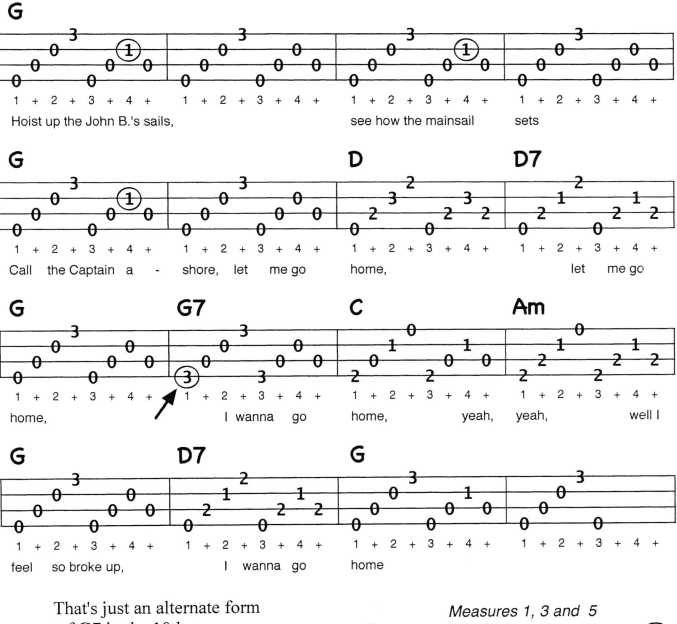

That's just an alternate form of **G7** in the 10th measure.

Next, add a *second* note to **Count 4**, Measures 1, 3 and 5 and **pinch** the 4th and 2nd strings between Thumb and Middle finger simultaneously. It's just an alternate form of **C**.

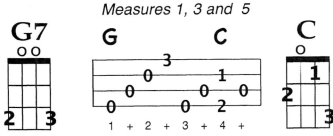

Measures 1, 3 and 5

2. Arpeggios in 3/4

Back to **3/4 Time**, where the counts are "One - & - Two - & - Three - &."
Here is *Morning Has Broken*. This first arpeggio, *Pattern #3*, starts by ascending with 4 notes like *Pattern #1*, then descending with 2 notes. As we go along, I'll keep introducing new chords, as well as new forms of old chords. "**Morning has...**"

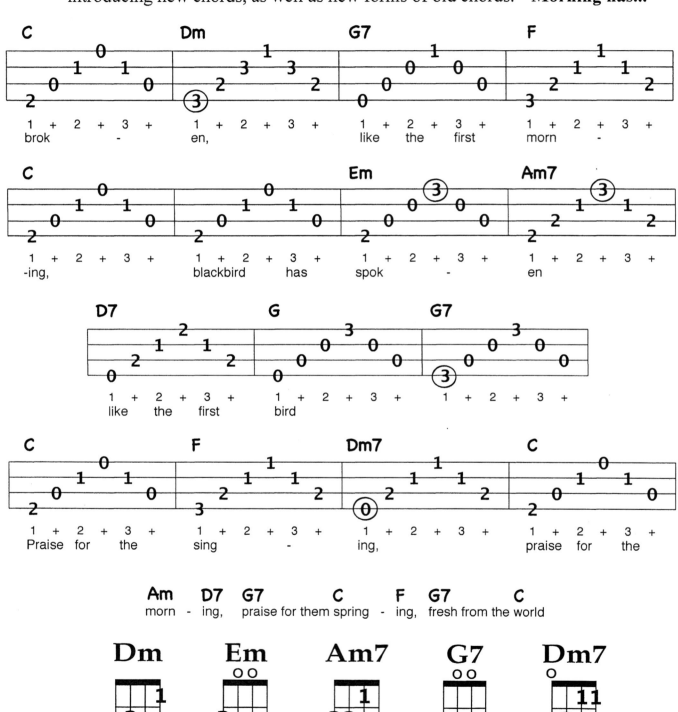

Amazing Grace is another tune in **3/4 Time**. Try the fetching, new ***Pattern #4***. This one **twins** (that's a verb) the Middle and Ring finger, pauses in the middle and twins them again. Watch for novel chord forms; *the whole second half has the 4th finger Anchored on the 1st string.*

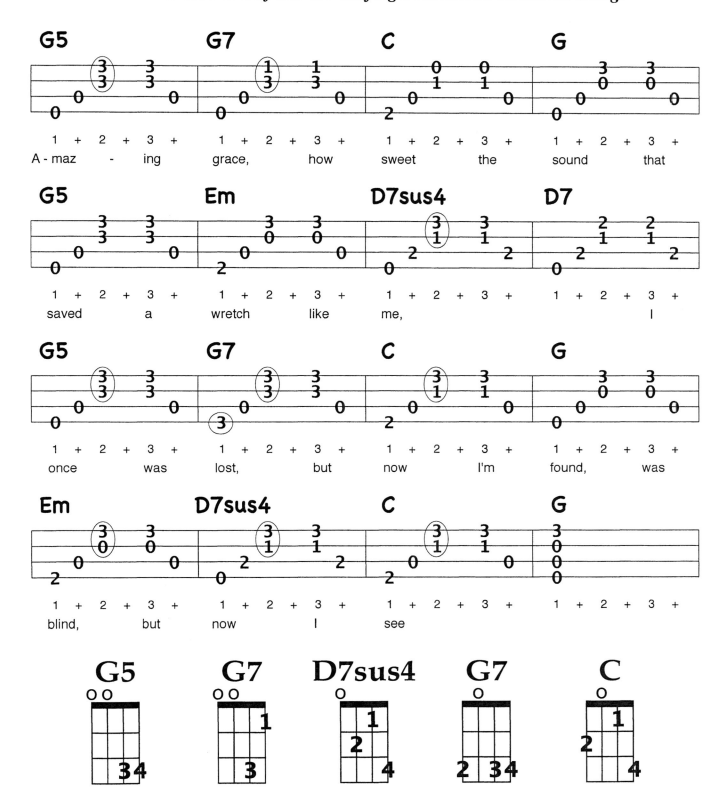

3. Travis Picking

Travis Picking, or Travis-Style playing, named after Merle Travis, is popular on the guitar, and there's no reason it can't work on the baritone ukulele. It's an alternating bass style, with a sort of ragtime, *boom-chicka* feel. The 3rd and 4th strings, though not particularly bassy, assume the role of the alternating bass, with the 2nd and 1st strings filling in. ***Pattern #5***:

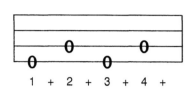

Hold down a **G** chord. Use the Thumb to alternate between the 4th and 3rd strings (to the left) *on the beats*. Then fill in with ***the Index finger on the 2nd string and the Middle finger on the 1st string*** (right). *Those finger notes come on the "+" counts.*

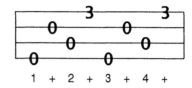

So the playing sequence is: **Thumb on 4th ... Index on 2nd ... Thumb on 3rd ... Middle on 1st**. Do that again, and you have one measure of Travis. Let's take a *(s-l-o-w)* whack at *Jingle Bells*:

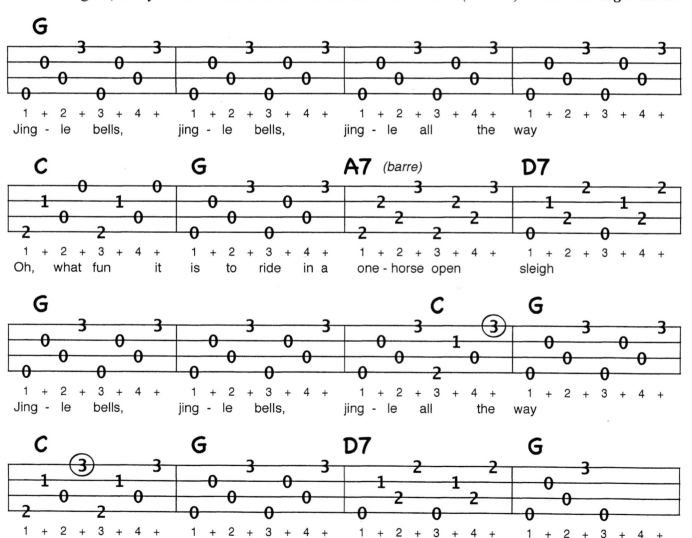

And here comes more of *Pattern #5* in *You Are My Sunshine*. Keep an eye out for unexpected fret changes. Again, pinkie stays put for a long time. "**You are my...**"

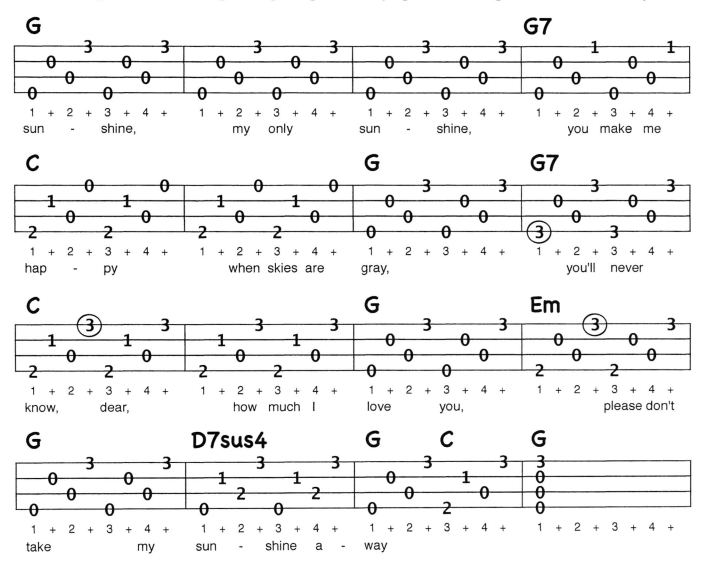

The Travis-Style Pinch Pattern

This next one, Pattern #6, is a bit trickier. You still keep the alternating bass with the Thumb: *Strings 4 - 3 - 4 - 3*. But now the Middle finger joins the Thumb on **Count 1** with a pinching motion, then you PAUSE and wait for **Count 2** to play the Thumb (on 3rd), followed by the Index finger (on 2nd) on **Count 2+**.

That's the first half of the pattern. I know, yikes!
But the second half is easier; you just play:
Thumb on 4th ... Middle on 1st
Thumb on 3rd ... Index on 2nd

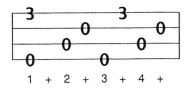

But you know what? Don't sweat *Pattern #6*. If it makes sense to you, great, but there's nothing wrong with sticking with *Pattern #5* for the rest of your life.

Five Foot Two finishes our tour of Travisville. Try both patterns. I'm giving you Fretboard Diagrams because I'm getting soft in my dottage.....dotage.

Scary Theory Part of the Book
a.k.a. Night of the Living Music Principles
a.k.a. String Theory from the Black Lagoon

Look, folks, there's nothing to fear but fear......*RUN! Save yourselves!*
Okay, let's take this discussion back to the level of the individual **note**.
Let's look again at the piano keyboard:

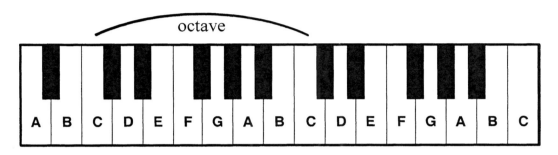

From before, you know that there are 7 different **natural** notes, the white keys, and 5 additional **accidental** notes, the black keys (verify that there are 5 black keys between the C notes, for example, which are 8 steps, or one **octave**, apart). Accidentals can be known either as **sharp** notes or **flat** notes; the black key farthest to the left can be called either A-sharp or B-flat, and for a good reason that is irrelevent right now. Let's eschew (bless you) the flat label in favor of the *sharp* label, so we'll be talking about natural notes (such as A) and sharps (such as A#).

The chords we have been playing are composed of these notes, which notes are organized into **scales**. The scale we like the most is called the **Major Scale**, and the Major Scale we like the most, from a music theory angle, is the **C Major Scale**. I've extracted one octave of the **C Major Scale** from the keyboard diagram:

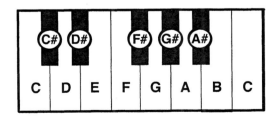

Now, if you play *only the white keys* from C to C, you'll have the **C Major Scale**, and it sounds exactly like the **Do - Re - Mi - Fa - Sol - La - Ti - Do** from *The Sound of Music*.

The C Chord Family

I want to show you how you can take the raw material of music, specifically the 12 notes in the Musical Alphabet as they are organized into Major Scales, and demonstrate *how to build all those chords we've been playing*. With that knowledge, you can go on to find and even create Your Own Chords to spice up your playing. I want to teach you to fish!

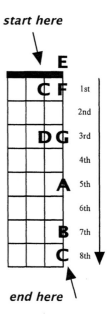

So there are 12 notes and therefore 12 Major Scales, each one starting on a different note. *Each Major Scale has a unique sequence of 7 notes, a subset of the 12, in some combination of natural and accidental notes, except for the C Major Scale, the only one that has All Natural Notes.*

Actually, on the baritone ukulele, the **C Major Scale** is not the best one for explaining music theory, because we don't get an entire octave of notes from the **C Major Scale** in **Open Position**, where we've been playing most of our chords. C'est la vie, mes amis, we're stuck with **C**. (At least play the chopped up scale to the right so you can hear the **Do - Re - Mi**.)

So we lay out all 12 notes in a row, starting with the C note and using sharps, not flats:

C - C# - D - D# - E - F - F# - G - G# - A - A# - B - C

This is called the **C Chromatic Scale**, but it's basically all 12 notes starting with C. Notice that there is no sharp from E to F (no E#) and no sharp from B to C (no B#).

We must extract the 7-note C Major Scale from the 12-note C Chromatic Scale. Luckily, *every major scale has the very same structure,* and you work it out using **Half-steps** and **Whole-steps**. A Half-step is the distance between two consecutive notes, so that's a Half-step from C to C#. A Whole-step is twice that, as from C to D.

The formula for any and every Major Scale is:

2 Whole-steps + 1 Half-step + 3 Whole-steps + 1 Half-step

If you never learn another blessed thing about music theory, *learn this!*
Sometimes this rule is shortened to *2 Wholes and a Half, 3 Wholes and a Half.*

The thing to do now is to apply this formula to the **C Chromatic Scale**.
I'll circle the notes that get picked off in the Whole-step/Half-step process:

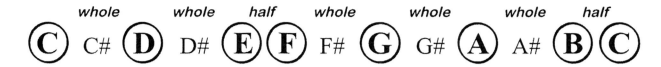

Well, durn! By sheer *dumb* luck, our formula picked off only the 7 white keys!
Of course, it's a set-up. For some reason "they" decided that **C** would be the key
whose Major Scale would fit exactly to the rule and produce all natural notes.
You can see most of the Whole- and Half-steps going up the neck on page 56.

*Scales are the most important sources of notes for playing melodies,
but we're going to keep examining the chord angle for the moment.*

So now that we have our scale, let's see how to generate the Chord Family,
so we can ***demonstrate*** which chords belong to the **Key of C**; in other words,
the chords we can expect to predominate in any song played in this key.

Once the 7 have been derived from the 12 (with one note, C, to rule them all),
we callously discard the other 5 and give them no additional consideration.
The remaining 7 receive equal weight regardless of how close they are
to each other (Whole-step or Half-step). Here they are, numbered:

C	D	E	F	G	A	B
1	2	3	4	5	6	7

You saw this yoking of letters and numbers before, when they represented *chords*
(**C** is the **1 chord, Dm** is the **2 chord**, and so on.) But now the letters represent single
notes and the numbers are **scale degrees**. Think of these as slots that are filled with
different notes from key to key. The sequence of notes is always the same
(it's alphabetical), but there will be different Root Notes and accidentals.

These individual notes will give rise to chords, specifically, ***the 3 Major chords,
the 3 Minor chords and the Diminished chord***, from the first part of the book.

What you do is to build TRIADS, which are 3-note structures. In fact,
they are **1 - 3 - 5** structures, *not* to be mixed up with all that **1 - 4 - 5** stuff:
"1, 3 and 5" are single notes, while *"1, 4 and 5" are fully formed chords.*

Here's the process: Take a note, say C, as the **1**. Skip the 2 (D) and choose the **3** (E).
Then skip the 4 (F) and choose the **5** (G). The **C** triad is spelled C - E - G. Duck soup.

So you apply this procedure to each note in turn, generating 7 triads.
Now, in order to grease the wheels of this jalopy, we'll need to lay out
one-and-a-half octaves of the **C Major Scale** (just the naturals, please).
Then starting from each chord's **Root Note** (the **1** of the **1 - 3 - 5**),
please observe that I am circling the notes of the triad:

Scale Degrees

		R	2	3	4	5	6	7	R	2	3	4		

1 chord   **C**   Ⓒ D Ⓔ F Ⓖ A B C D E F = **C - E - G**

2m chord   **Dm**   C Ⓓ E Ⓕ G Ⓐ B C D E F = **D - F - A**

3m chord   **Em**   C D Ⓔ F Ⓖ A Ⓑ C D E F = **E - G - B**

4 chord   **F**   C D E Ⓕ G Ⓐ B Ⓒ D E F = **F - A - C**

5 chord   **G**   C D E F Ⓖ A Ⓑ C Ⓓ E F = **G - B - D**

6m chord   **Am**   C D E F G Ⓐ B Ⓒ D Ⓔ F = **A - C - E**

7dim chord   **Bdim**   C D E F G A Ⓑ C Ⓓ E Ⓕ = **B - D - F**

Every triad has a **1 - 3 - 5** structure, or a **Root**, a **3rd** and a **5th**.
Collectively these are known as the **Chord Tones** of a given triad,
and they contribute in different ways to the sound of the chord:

The triad's **Root Note** is the foundational note of the chord.
It holds up the rest of the chord the way a root holds up a plant.
That's why the chord is named after the **Root Note**. It is *Captain Kirk*.

The **5th** is another strong note, but is subsidiary to the **Root**.
It contributes to the structure of the chord...solid...stoic...cerebral.
The **Root** and **5th** together form a mighty team. The **5th** is *Mr. Spock*.

But the **3rd** is where the heart is. It adds the warmth and personality,
and it determines whether the chord sounds Happy Major or Sad Minor.
It is *Dr. Leonard H. "Bones" McCoy*. It's *Triad Trek! In color!*

So now we've established that the **C Major Triad** is spelled C - E - G.
We want to track down the C, E and G notes that lie all over the fretboard
so that we can find different locations of the **C Major** chord. You've been playing
a sort of default, standard **C** chord in Open Position, the one that I *told* you to play,
but it's not your only choice; let's see what else is available around the fretboard.

The Fretboard Diagram on the left shows the locations of all the notes in
the **C Major Scale** across the 4 strings and up through the 10th fret. (You know,
the 4th string is an open D note, and then there's a Whole-step to the E note, then
a Half-step to the F note, etc., just as you saw above.) Since this is the **Key of C**,
these are all the natural notes, no sharps. The next diagram retains only
the Chord Tones, C, E and G, and loses the other notes (D, F, A, B).

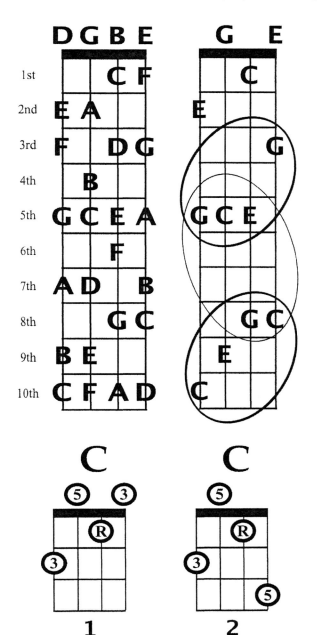

So if we are seeking other positions on
the neck for playing the **C** chord, we just
identify the spots where the chord tones
cluster into shapes that we can finger.
And notice that these shapes overlap.

I've pulled out the most playable shapes
for the **C** chord and numbered them **1** to **5**
(below and on the next page). The dots in
the diagrams are now labeled **R**, **3** and **5**,
for the 3 Chord Tones of the **C** chord.

The first **C** chord below, **#1**, is our Default **C**.
It has a **Root**, a **5th** and *two* **3rds**, and one of
those **3rds** is in the **bass** (on the lowest, or
4th string). ***Whatever note you find in the
bass adds a lot to the coloring of the chord***,
so it is the warm and soft **3rd** that really
predominates *in this particular shape*.

C chord **#2** stays in Open Position and adds
either the 3rd or 4th finger to the G note on
the 1st string. So we are swapping that **3rd**
in #1 for a **5th**, which makes this shape
stronger than **#1**. Also makes a nice
Anchor to a **G** chord.

*Remember, the numbers in the diagrams
are now **Chord Tones**, not fingerings.*

Now we go up the neck. I've circled the note clusters in the diagram on the last page that can be most easily fingered. Each of these note clusters is a genu-wine C chord; it just won't *look* like the C chord you are used to playing. In fact, ***you should expect these clusters to resemble some of the other chord shapes that you've been playing***.

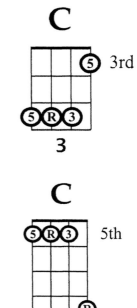

What do you make of **C** chord **#3**? This chord is in what is called **3rd Position**, because the 1st finger is placed at the 3rd fret. And it *looks* like the **B** chord that we saw back in the **Key of E** on page 30, only one fret higher. It has a **Root**, a **3rd** and *two* **5ths**, with one of those **5ths** in the bass, where it has greater influence over the sound of the chord. So this shape is more *5thy* and sounds stronger than either **C** chord **#1** or **#2**.

#4 resembles a **G** chord if you imagine the barre at the 5th fret to be the *nut* of the uke. It has the same 5th in the bass as **#3**, but it has *two* **Roots**, making it the strongest **C** so far.

But look at **#5**, which has the shape of the Default **F** chord in 8th Position and is also equipped with two **Roots**, but one of them is *in the bass*, where notes have the greatest influence. This is the **C** chord with the strongest shape, when you consider the internal layout of the notes, though it is a bit high in pitch.

. . . .

You may ask me, Why am I doing this to you? Why can't I just leave you alone and let you play the friendly, simple **C** chord that you have come to love and depend on?

Perhaps the simple **C** will keep you satisfied for a *l-o-n-g* time, maybe forever. But I'm looking ahead to the day that you find yourself a little antsy with the old and ready for the new. It can happen. So I'm going to soldier onward and show you more chords up the neck.

But first I want to reveal to you the Grand Overview, the blueprint, the key that unlocks the fretboard: *It's all based on the **C-A-G-E-D** System.* After you've been through this, if you would like a more in-depth discussion of the ***C-A-G-E-D*** System, check out my ***Music Principles for the Skeptical Guitarist*** series and ignore the 5th and 6th strings.

The Five C - A - G - E - D Chord Forms

I keep alluding to the fact that most of the chords on the ukulele can be traced back to one of *5 different chord shapes*. They are *C - A - G - E - D*.

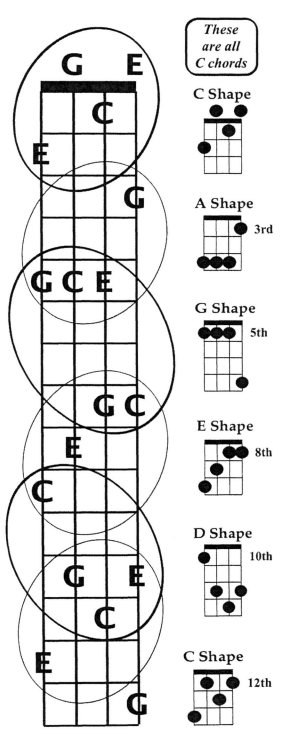

You might have thought that there is an **F** shape, but the **F** chord is actually a version of the **E** shape set at the 1st fret. Just imagine a barre all the way across the lowest note fretted in a chord and look at what's left:

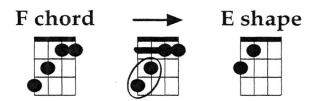

This is also true of the **B** chord, which actually has an **A** shape:

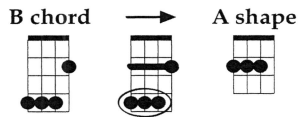

And no matter what the chord, these shapes always occur up the neck in the same sequence: C-A-G-E-D-C-A-G-E-D, to infinity and beyond.

Look at the long diagram. I extended it several more frets so you could see where the sequence starts over, even though we can't make the reach.

And the consecutive shapes always OVERLAP by one, two or three notes (check the circles).

*All this is true for **all keys**. The A shape always follows the C shape, G always follows A, and so on. **The same sequence, just different starting chords.***

Now that we've done the **1 chord**, C, let's go on to the **4** and **5** chords, **F** and **G**. I'll show you just the Chord Tones from each of the two triads and locate the note clusters that can be turned into playable chord shapes.

The **F Major Triad** includes the F, A and C notes, and that's all you see on the neck diagram to the left, and here are the overlapping playable shapes:

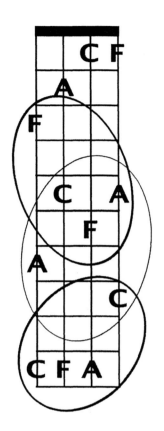
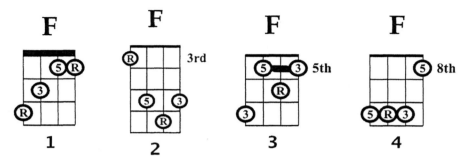

The 4 chord shapes for **F** are **E-D-C-A** (from *C-A-G-**E-D-C-A**-G-E-D*).

#1 is our Default **F**, a strong sounding **E** chord shape.
#2 has the **D** chord shape, if you place a barre at the 3rd fret, and it's just as strong as #1 (*two* **Roots**, one in the bass), though it is pitched a bit higher. *This one is hard to finger, but you can omit the* **Root** *on the 2nd string if you use your 1st, 3rd and 4th fingers, and* **mute** *the 2nd string with your 3rd finger (see below).*

#3 has the **C** shape, played with a barre at the 5th fret, and #4 has the **A** shape, imagining a barre at the 8th fret. *Now, play these 4 pairs of C and F chords, and you'll see the variety that we've uncovered:*

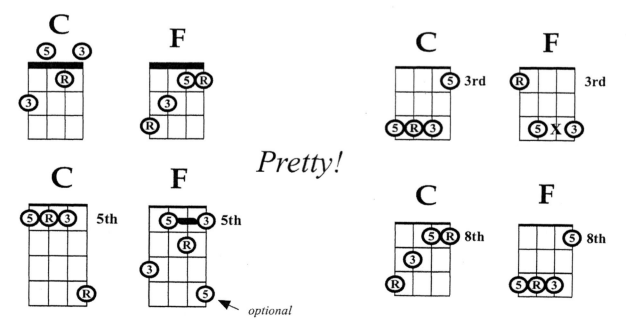

Pretty!

You've got 4 pairs of bona fide **C** and **F** chords scattered about the neck that have different internal arrangements of the notes that make them sound *different but the same*, sort of the way in which two octaves of the same note sound different but the same. You know, you have the whole neck, use it!

The first pair is the Default **C** and **F**. The second pair, to the right, uses that modified **F** chord with the **D** shape that deadens the 2nd string, at the **X**. The **F** chord in the third pair (**C** shape) has an optional pinky note; looks like **C** chord #2. The **F** chord in the fourth pair (**A** shape) is too crowded for me to squeeze my big fat fingers in there. Good luck yourself.

. . . .

The **G Major Triad** includes the G, B and D notes, and that's all you see on the neck diagram to the left, and here are the overlapping playable shapes:

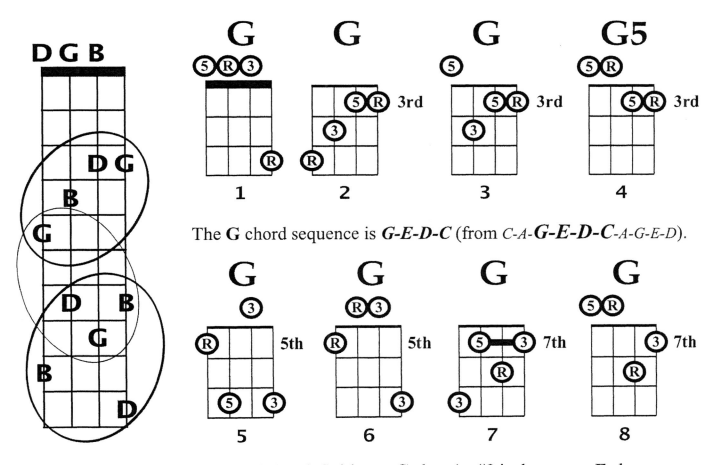

The G chord sequence is *G-E-D-C* (from *C-A-**G-E-D-C**-A-G-E-D*).

Briefly, #1 is the Default **G** (by definition, a **G** shape). #2 is the strong **E** shape. #3 is like #2 except that it has an open 4th string, a **D** note, a **5th** instead of a **Root**, so that #3 is not as strong. But #4 is what is known as a **Power Chord**; no soft **3rds**, two open strings---*strongest*. The chord symbol is **G5**, indicating **Roots** and **5ths** only. #5 (a **D** shape) uses one open string (or you can mute it) and #6 uses two of them. #7 has the shape of the Default **C**, and #8 is a piece of #7 with two open strings.

Play *La Bamba*, with the straight **1 - 4 - 5** progression, at the following 4 positions.

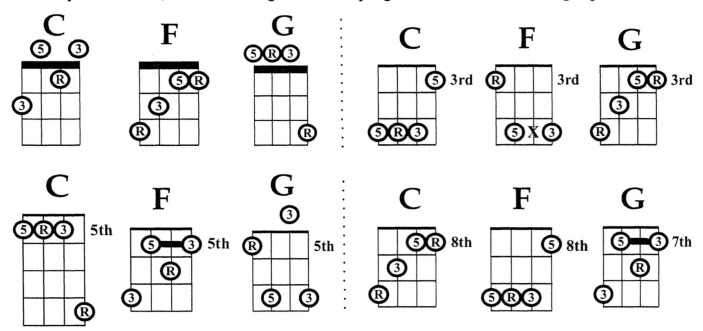

You can decide if you like any or all of these. The first three stay within their positions, and the last one moves up and down the neck a little.

While we're at it, we should check out some different possibilities for the **G7** chord. ***The G7 chord is an example of a quadrad, with 4 notes instead of 3.*** It's simple, really, just go **1 - 3 - 5 - 7** to pick off the extra note. Go back to page 58, take the **G** triad and find the 7th note, F. So the **G7** quadrad is spelled G - B - D - F. So we add two F notes, an octave apart, to the **G** diagram.

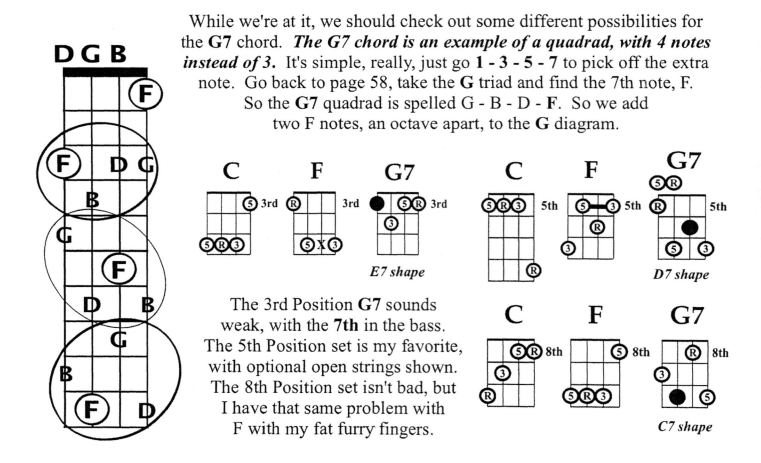

The 3rd Position **G7** sounds weak, with the **7th** in the bass. The 5th Position set is my favorite, with optional open strings shown. The 8th Position set isn't bad, but I have that same problem with F with my fat furry fingers.

Big Uke vs. Small Uke: What's the Dif?

We can use this *C-A-G-E-D* business to explain the musical difference between the baritone ukulele and the soprano/concert/tenor family of smaller ukes.

The baritone uke is tuned **D - G - B - E**. This is called **G6 Tuning** because when you play these 4 notes together, you sound a **G6** chord (find **G6** in middle of page 86).

If you go up each of these strings chromatically, one note/one fret at a time, to the 5th fret, you find the notes **G - C - E - A**.

Well, that just happens to be C6 Tuning, the tuning for the small ukes.

So if you saw off the bari-uke at the 5th fret, or, more practically, put a capo (clamp) across the 5th fret, you've got yourself a *de facto* small uke.

Except that most small ukes have their 4th strings tuned to a G note that is ***one octave higher*** than you'd expect. This is the "My Dog Has Fleas" device used to tune small ukes. It's called Reentrant Tuning.

This is why Small Ukers call the baritone **G** chord a **C** chord: It's our ***G shaped C chord*** at the 5th fret.

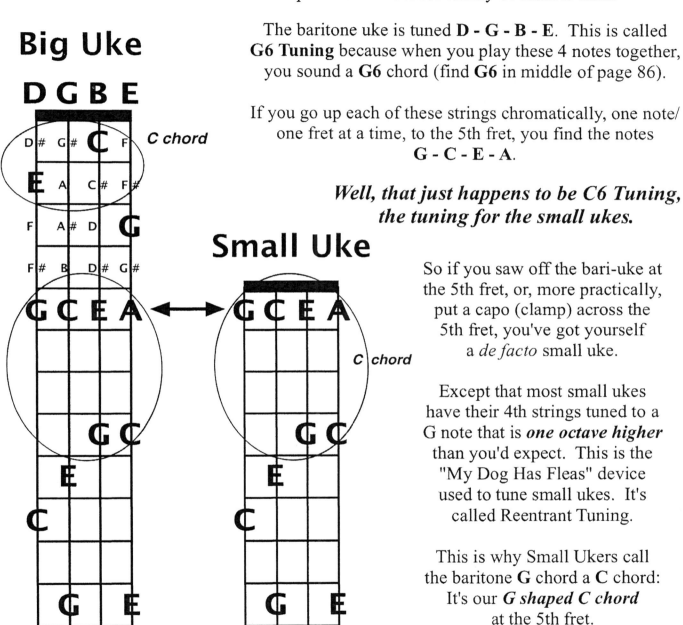

Baritone G   **Soprano C**

*If you are reading song sheets with chord diagrams written for small ukes, play the **name** of the chord, not the shape.*

65

The G Chord Family

As you know by now, **FIVE** is a sort of magic number in music that is the core of the phenomenon known as the **Circle of Fifths**. *Count up an interval of a 5th from C to find G*. So the **G Chord Family** is the next stop in our exploration of musical keys.

Here's the **G Chromatic Scale**, which is all the notes laid out from G to G:

G - G# - A - A# - B - C - C# - D - D# - E - F - F# - G

We pick off the notes for the **G Major Scale** using our formula: **W-W-H-W-W-W-H**:

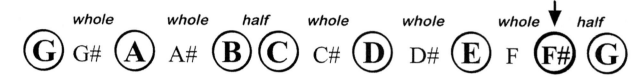

But a funny thing has happened on the way to the **G Chord Family**: *We've picked up one of those accidentals that we've been tiptoeing around.*

This may seem like a small thing, but it's BIG. Think about it: *If you change one note in the scale, you change three chords in the key, because every note appears as a Root, a 3rd or a 5th in three different triads.*

Let's run through the new triad-building procedure with our new friend, F#. Behold:

```
                    Scale Degrees
               R  2  3  4  5  6  7  R  2  3  4

1 chord     G      Ⓖ A Ⓑ C Ⓓ E F#  G  A  B  C   =   G - B - D

2m chord    Am     G Ⓐ B Ⓒ D Ⓔ F#  G  A  B  C   =   A - C - E

3m chord    Bm     G A Ⓑ C Ⓓ E Ⓕ# G  A  B  C   =   B - D - F#

4 chord     C      G A B Ⓒ D Ⓔ F# Ⓖ A  B  C   =   C - E - G

5 chord     D      G A B C Ⓓ E Ⓕ# G Ⓐ B  C   =   D - F# - A

6m chord    Em     G A B C D Ⓔ F# Ⓖ A Ⓑ C   =   E - G - B

7dim chord  F#dim  G A B C D E Ⓕ# G Ⓐ B Ⓒ   =   F# - A - C
```

The presence of the F# note creates 3 new chords for the **G Chord Family**:
Bm (B-D-F#) ...... **D** (D-F#-A) ...... **F#dim** (F#-A-C).

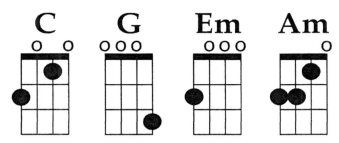

The remaining 4 chords (to the right) belong to *both* the **Key of C** and **Key of G**, as they contain *only* notes common to both, because they bear neither an F nor an F#.

As you well know, the Major chords in the **Key of G**, the **1 - 4 - 5's**, are **G - C - D**.
Since we already found all the C and G chords on the neck back in the Key of C, all we need to do now is to find the D chords (**Bm** comes later, **F#dim** not at all).

We need a slightly altered Fretboard Diagram for the new
Key of G, *one that bears F# notes instead of F notes:*

Now that you know about the *C-A-G-E-D* sequence of chord shapes up the neck, you won't be surprised to see the Default **D** chord followed by the **C** shape, **A** shape and **G** shape (**D-C-A-G**).

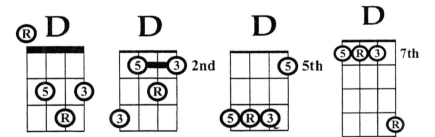

But there's something else we can take advantage of here: *the Root D note on the open 4th string. The low Root makes these variants stronger, and the open string makes them more fun to play.*

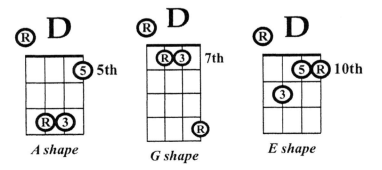

67

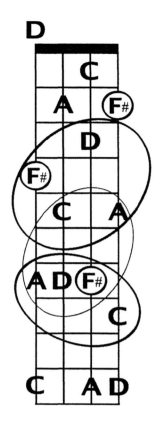

Ah, but let's not forget about the **D7** chord, the more restless version of the **5 chord** in the **Key of G**. As was the **G7** chord in the **Key of C**, the **D7** chord here is a quadrad, a **1 - 3 - 5 - 7** structure. Go back to page 66 and pick off the 7th note from the D note and find D - F# - A - C, track down the C notes in the diagram to the left and build your **D7** chords:

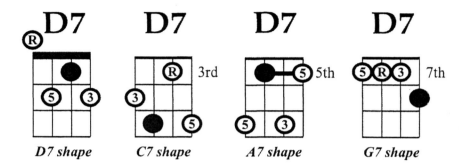

All these but the 3rd one have all 4 Chord Tones, while the 3rd one has a **3rd**, two **5ths** and no **Roots** (a little unsettling, that.)

And we can do the same trick, keeping the 4th string open, as you can see in these **1 - 4 - 5** progressions in 4 positions:

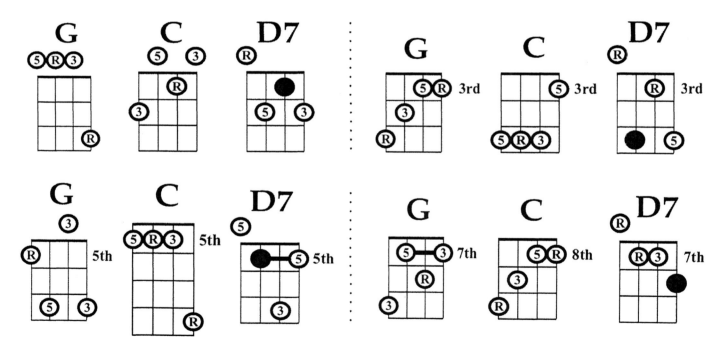

You're probably getting the idea of the patterns involved in playing **1 - 4 - 5** progressions around the neck, but I want to drag you through *one more key*, **D**, which has 2 sharps.

The D Chord Family

69

From the **Key of G**, you proceed up a 5th to find the **Key of D**.
Here's the **D Chromatic Scale**, which is all the notes laid out from D to D:

D - D# - E - F - F# - G - G# - A - A# - B - C - C# - D

We pick off the notes for the **D Major Scale** using our formula: **W-W-H-W-W-W-H**:

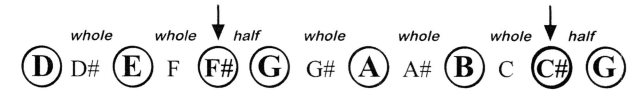

What have we here? Looks like we've retained the F# from the **Key of G** and added a second sharp, C#. By the way, the more sharps we add in moving from key to key, the fewer chords we'll expect to find in common with the all-natural **Key of C**.

See, the **Key of C** and the **Key of G** differ by one sharp, F#, and the **Key of G** and the **Key of D** differ by one sharp, C#. *But the Keys of C and D differ by both sharps.* From the standpoint of the **C Chord Family**, the **G Chord Family** are like first cousins, but the **D Chord Family** are like your cousins' *cousins*; related, but not as closely.

And we have uncovered a significant music principle: ***Starting from the Key of C, every time you move up an interval of a 5th, you find a key with one additional sharp.*** Proceeding around the Circle of Fifths *clockwise* gives us: **C - G - D - A - E - B - F#**.....

So let's work out the chords that comprise the **D Chord Family**, with 2 sharps, F# and C#:

1 chord	D	(D) E (F#) G (A) B C# D E F# G	= **D - F# - A**
2m chord	Em	D (E) F# (G) A (B) C# D E F# G	= **E - G - B**
3m chord	F#m	D E (F#) G (A) B (C#) D E F# G	= **F# - A - C#**
4 chord	G	D E F# (G) A (B) C# (D) E F# G	= **G - B - D**
5 chord	A	D E F# G (A) B (C#) D (E) F# G	= **A - C# - E**
6m chord	Bm	D E F# G A (B) C# (D) E (F#) G	= **B - D - F#**
7dim chord	C#dim	D E F# G A B (C#) D (E) F# (G)	= **C# - E - G**

The presence of the C# note creates 3 new chords for the **D Chord Family**:
F#m (F#-A-C#) ...... **A** (A-C#-E) ...... **C#dim** (C#-E-G).

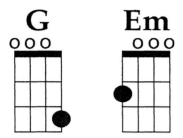

But from the angle of the *C Chord Family*, there are only *2 chords left* that it shares with the **D Chord Family**, **G** and **Em**. Neither of these chords contains any F- or C-type notes.

As you well know, the Major chords in the **Key of D**, the 1 - 4 - 5's, are **D - G - A**. Since we've already tracked down all the **D** and **G** chords on the neck, our task now is to find the **A** chords (we'll look at the **F#m** chord later and the **C#dim** not at all).

We need a slightly altered Fretboard Diagram for the new **Key of D**, *one that bears F# notes instead of F notes and C# notes instead of C notes:*

Look at the shapes of the **A** Chord Tones as you progress up the neck. You can see the last 4 letters of the word *(C-)A-G-E-D* in the sequence. Remember, the **F** shape is really an **E** shape, and the 4th chord would look more like a **D** shape if we hadn't blocked the 2nd string and cut out that note.

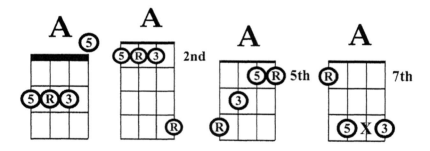

Let's briefly throw in the G note that serves as the **7th** note of the A7 quadrad (A - C# - E - G) and discover our A7 chords up the neck *(A-G-E-D)*:

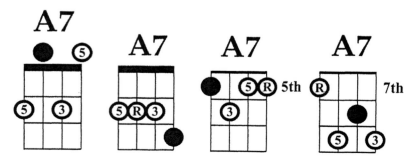

Now for the **1 - 4 - 5 chord** progressions in the **Key of D**:

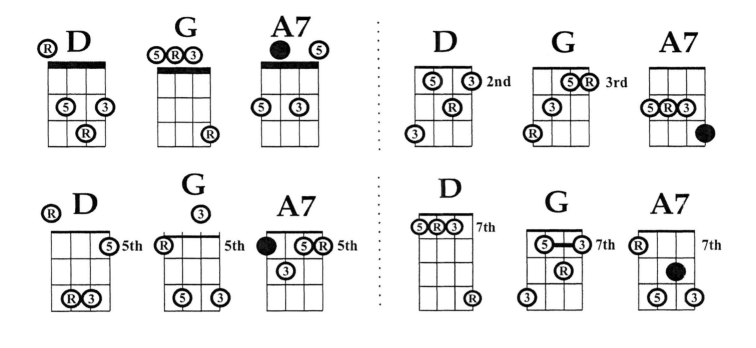

Our Three Overlapping Keys

I hope this little chart is more helpful than it is vexing. I just want to give you *The Big Picture* of what is going on around here.

The 1st column is the **C Chord Family**, and I have *circled* the 4 chords that it shares with the **G Chord Family** in the 2nd column:
C - Em - G - Am

Skip to the *3rd* column, **D Chord Family**, where I have *boxed in* the 4 chords that it shares with the **G Chord Family** in the 2nd column:
D - Em - G - Bm

The only two chords that **G** shares with *both* **C** and **D** are *circled and boxed*:
G - Em

Key of C	*Key of G*	*Key of D*
(C)	[G]	D
Dm	Am	Em
(Em)	Bm	F#m
F	(C)	G
(G)	D	A
(Am)	[Em]	Bm
Bdim	F#dim	C#dim

To put that more succinctly:

The **Keys of C and G**, which are a **5th** apart and differ by 1 sharp, share 4 chords.
The **Keys of G and D**, which are a **5th** apart and differ by 1 sharp, share 4 chords.
But the **Keys of C and D**, which are two **5ths** apart, share only 2 chords.
Ergo: *One sharp different = 4 chords in common + 3 not.*

Two more keys: **A** is up a **5th** from **D** and **E** is up a **5th** from **A**. The Circle of Fifths (review page 42) shows us that the **Key of A** is next (with 3 sharps, adding G#), then the **Key of E** (with 4 sharps, adding D#), completing the segment of the Circle we care most about: **C - G - D - A - E**. Let's skip the details of creating the **1 - 4 - 5's** and just consider the results:

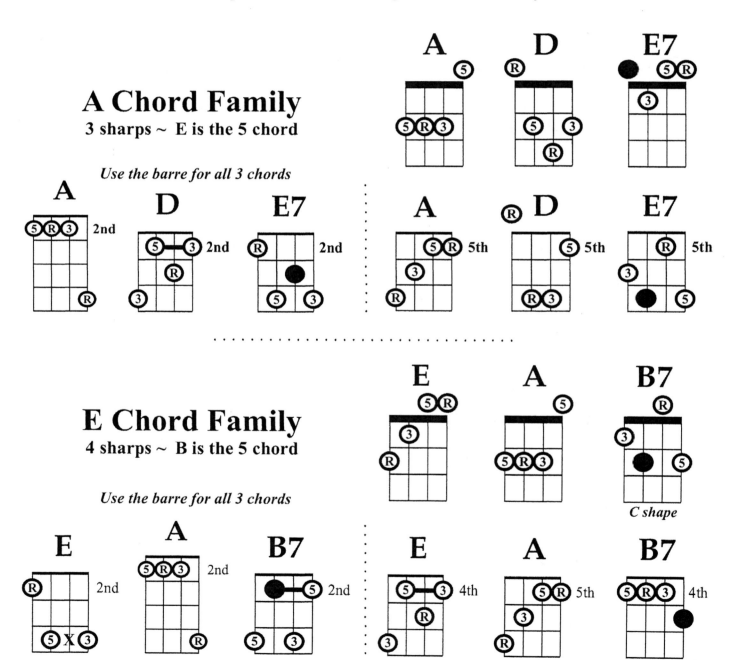

Minor Chords

73

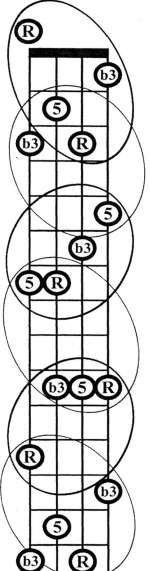

It might not surprise you to learn that the Minor chords follow the same C-A-G-E-D chord shape pattern moving up the neck.

The diagram to the left takes as an example the **Dm** chords progressing up the neck. It's just the same as the **D Major** diagram except that *all the 3rds are flatted*.

In fact, the only difference between any Major and Minor chord having the same letter name is whether the chord contains a Regular (Major) 3rd or a Flatted (Minor) 3rd.

So here are the 5 Minor chord shapes starting with **D** and progressing through the rest of the shapes (I put tiny circles on the Major **3rds**).

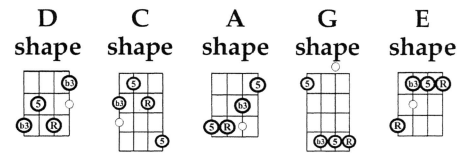

As it happens, we don't much like the **C** and **G** shape Minors chords, so I'll skip them below. The **Dm** chords will retain the **Root Note** on the open 4th string:

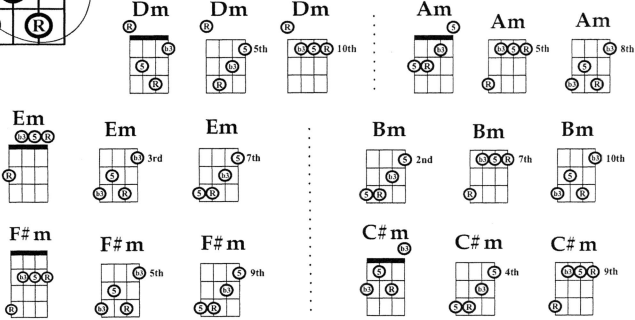

Our Songs All Over the Neck

Time to put some of the results of this high-faluting technical analysis to use.

You are probably pretty good at strumming now, and making headway with your fingerpicking. So far, we have just been playing an accompaniment style, where a voice or another instrument is taking the melody and the uke is providing backup.

What I want to do now is twofold:

(1) Use some of these new chords around the neck in some of Our Songs, and
(2) Add **melody** notes to play over the chords to create **instrumental renditions**.

You can simply strum or fingerpick just the chords---I'll provide Chord Diagrams for the specific shapes and chord voicings you'll need. OR you can try your hand at the next level by combining the melody with the chords, using either
(1) your fingers or (2) a pick in a pick/strum style.

The simplest way I know to express individual musical notes is to revisit our old friend, the Tab Diagram, where a number on a line represents the *fret number on a string* that you're being asked to play.

Here's a piece of Tab that gives you the first line of *Five Foot Two* in the **Key of C**:

```
─0───3───0─────┬─0───4───0─────┬─0───5───0───5─┬─0───5───0───5─
───────────────┼───────────────┼───────────────┼───────────────
───────────────┼───────────────┼───────────────┼───────────────
───────────────┴───────────────┴───────────────┴───────────────
 1 + 2 + 3 + 4 + 1 + 2 + 3 + 4 + 1 + 2 + 3 + 4 + 1 + 2 + 3 + 4 +
```

It's all on the *1st string* (the thinnest, the highest in pitch and nearest the floor), and varies between the open, 3rd, 4th and 5th frets. I'm using this tune as an example because of the number "**5**," to help remind you that these are not *finger* numbers but **FRET** numbers, since we use only 4 fingers to form the notes, not all 5.

You Are My Sunshine (in the **Key of D**) sports melody notes on the first 3 strings, starting on the 3rd string. *Here, we also add the chord tones of the D chord and contrast them with the melody notes in a slightly smaller and lighter font:*

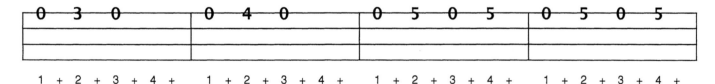

```
 1 + 2 + 3 + 4 + 1 + 2 + 3 + 4 + 1 + 2 + 3 + 4 + 1 + 2 + 3 + 4 +
```

Amazing Grace *in the Key of C*

75

Look at the Chord Diagram first. What'd he say? **Look at the Chord Diagram first.**
Hold each chord as long as you can before moving on: (1) it's prettier when the notes ring longer, and (2) you might *already be holding* the next note you need, you never know. And if you encounter an open circle in a Chord Diagram, you'll be able to add that note *while retaining the current chord*. Melody notes will be in **bold** type, others lighter.

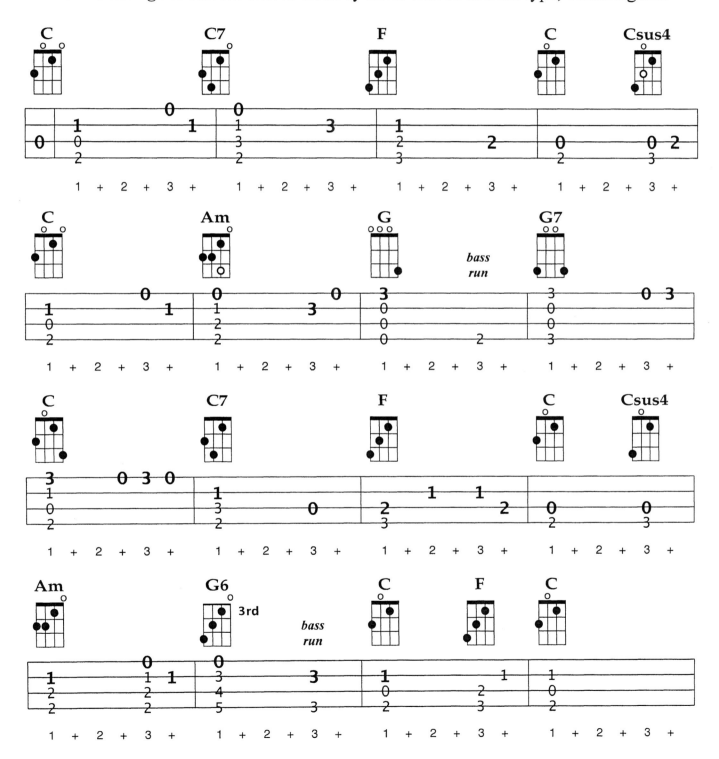

Amazing Grace in the Key of D

This arrangement is up two keys from **C**, and I think it sounds good to play the first verse in the **Key of C** and the second verse in the **Key of D**---uplifting! It's more efficient if you can maintain that barre for the first two chords in Line 3 and just move your pinkie around, but you can always fall back to a default **D**.

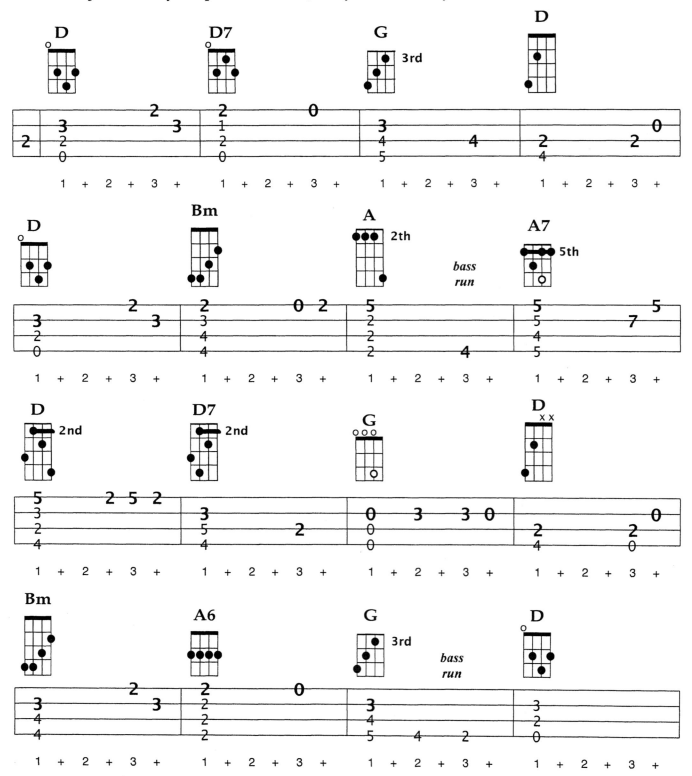

Amazing Grace *in the Key of G*

This arrangement heads up the neck right away and spends about half its time there. And I think it makes a nice 3rd verse---start in the **Key of C**, move to the **Key of D** and finish here in the **Key of G**. Sounds professional! That 2nd **Em** chord in the last line is sort of optional, but at least nail the "7" as a single note.

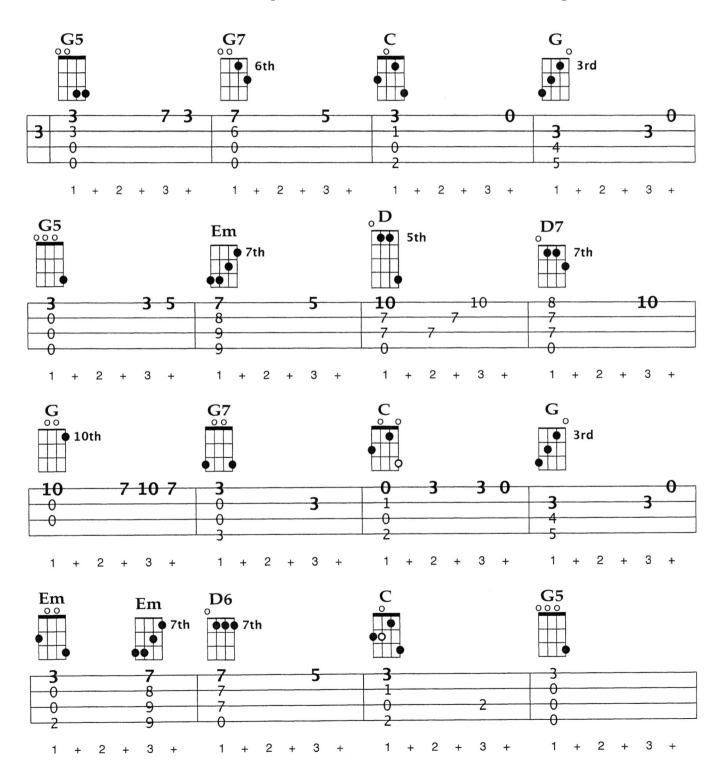

Morning Has Broken in the Key of C

Remember to hang onto the chords as long as you can without losing the beat.
I have an "**X**" over the 1st string in the **G5**; it would obscure the melody if played.
In fact, for that very reason, it's best in general to limit the **harmony notes**
(Chord Tones) to the strings below [in pitch] the melody notes.

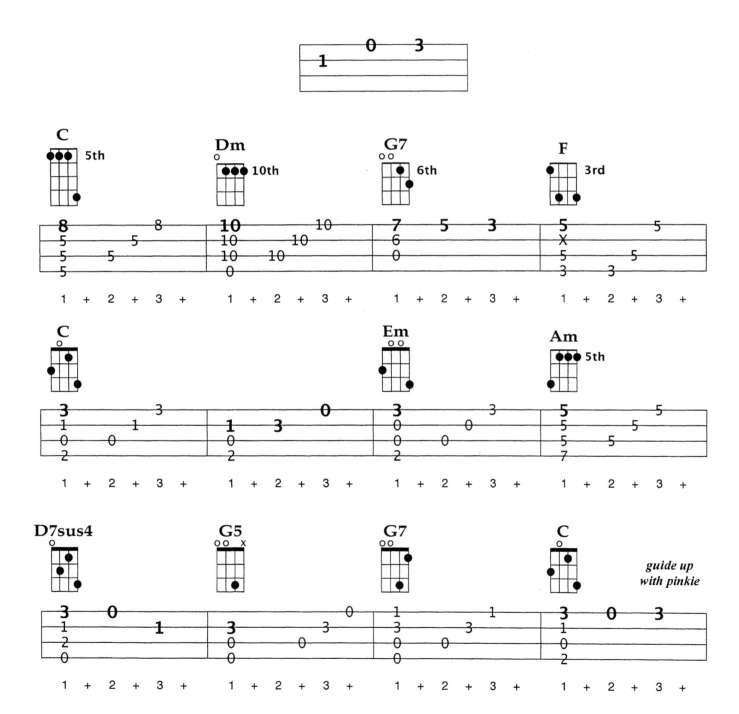

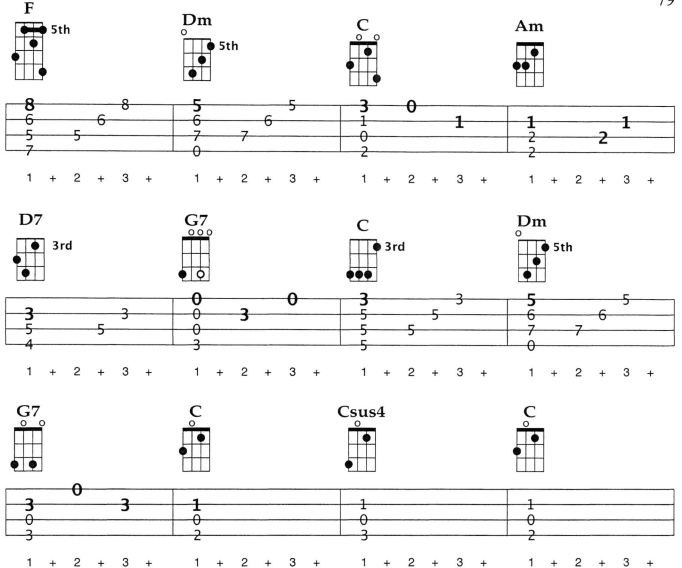

I wonder how all this is going for you. If you have chosen to ignore the Tab and just strum and sing, more power to you. You'll still impress your playmates. If you do strum, don't let an open 1st string ring over a melody note (mute it).

If you ARE playing the Tab, by pick or by finger, what you are actually doing is a simplified version of what the jazz players call **chord-melody** playing. We're doing chord changes mainly on the first beat of each measure, but you could theoretically change chords on every single melody note---lotsa chord changing.

Sometimes the same note will function first as a melody note and then as a harmony note in the same measure, so you'll see it first boldly then lightly. All those arpeggios are there to beef up the sound, of course. Pretty boring without them, but you can experiment with different patterns, if you are adventurous. Make up your own.

Auld Lang Syne *in the Key of D*

There are several opportunities here for using Guide Fingers, which make it so much easier to get around the fretboard. I've marked the spots and named the fingers involved.

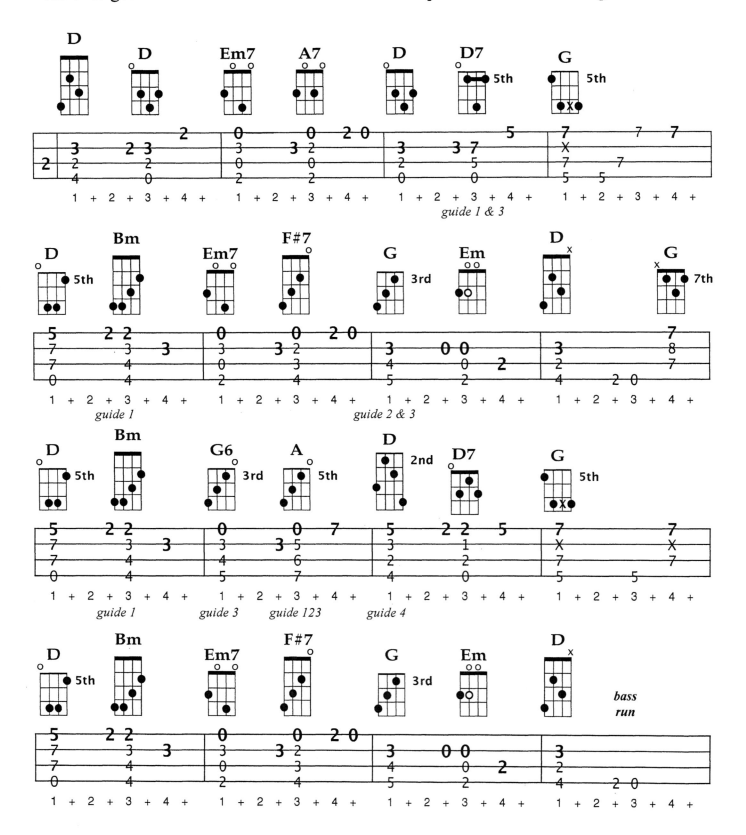

Jingle Bells *in the Key of C*

Here's the first of 4 Travis-Style arrangements. Remember, the open circles are notes that you can add while continuing to hold the chord. The 3rd and 4th lines incorporate some of the melody notes into the Travis-Style Pinch Pattern (#6), which removes them from their usual spots in the melody.

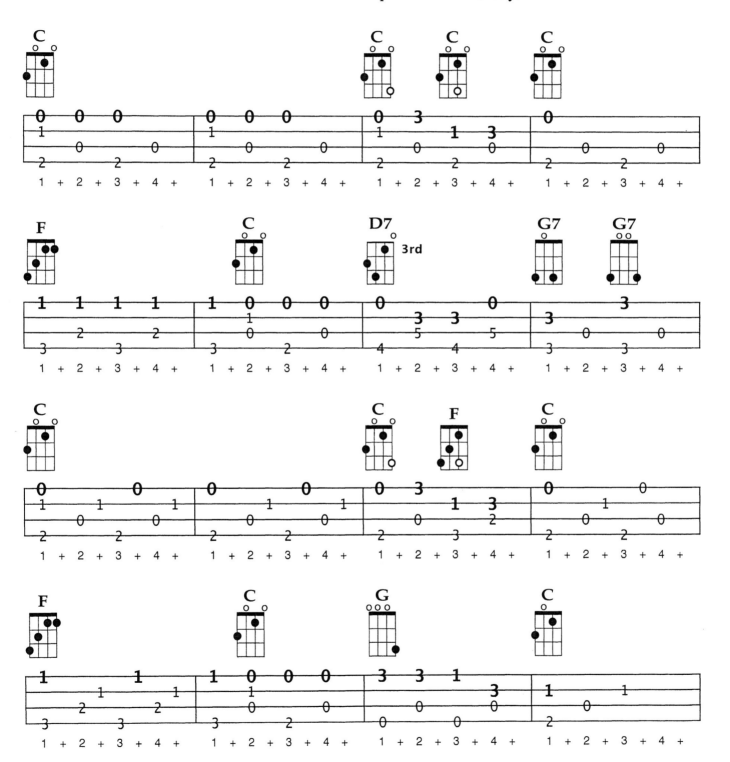

You Are My Sunshine *in the Key of D*

On Line 1, Measure 2, just lower the whole **D** chord by one fret on **Count 3**, then move it back up on **Count 4**. On Line 2, keep your Thumb moving as the melody rises and falls. On Line 3, Measure 2, **Counts 3** and **4**, those are descending intervals of a **3rd**; if you have trouble keeping the Thumb going, leave it out, but be sure to play those **3rds**.

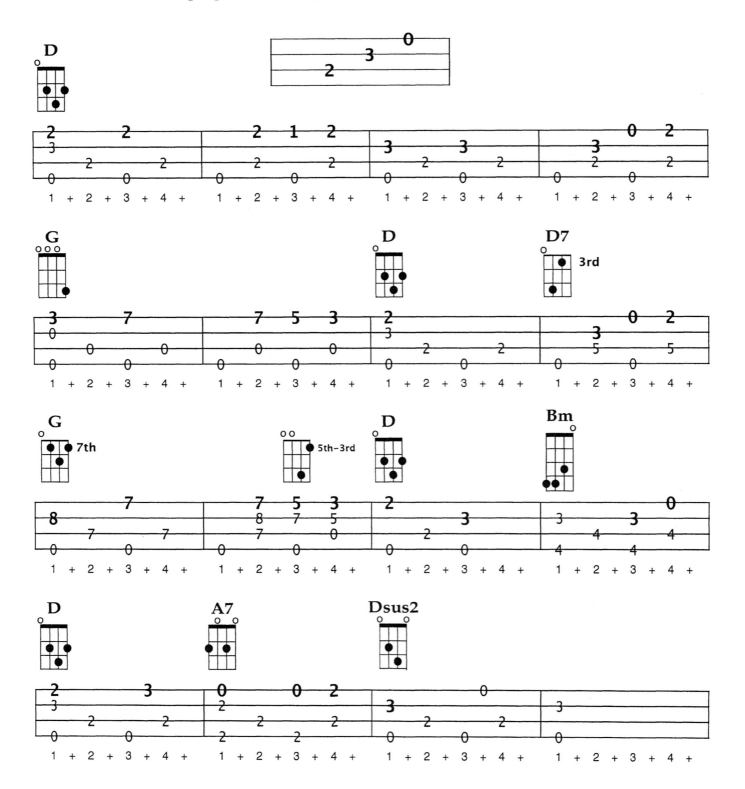

Ain't She Sweet *in the Key of C*

The final two Travis pieces are about equally challenging, so if you are struggling with one, try the other one. They both contain more barre chords around the neck, more picking pattern notes between the beats, and occasional **syncopated** notes, which are *melody* notes that are offset from the beat. There are also several stretches where the bass pattern pulls back, leaving only the melody.

Verse

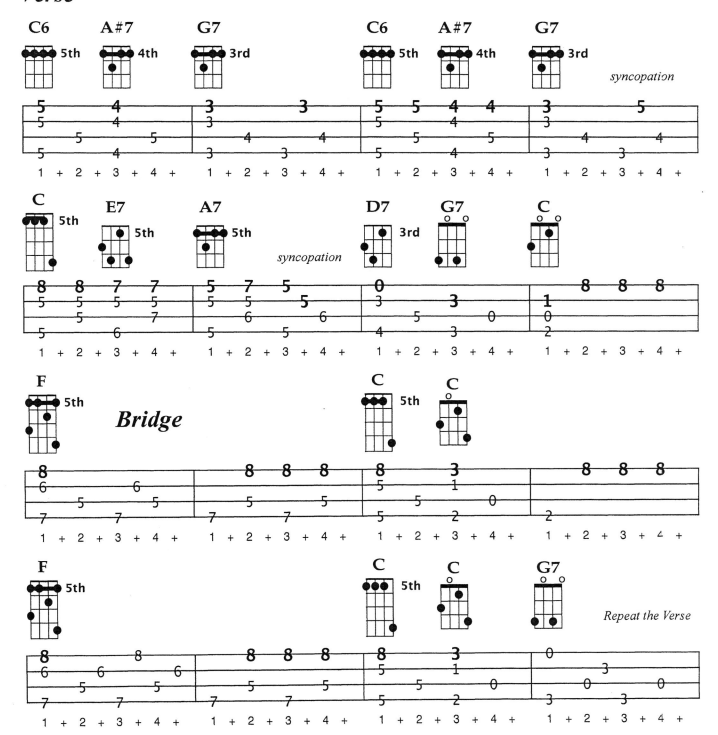

Five Foot Two in the Key of C

The second chord of each verse is a different form of **E/E7** each time, so keep checking.

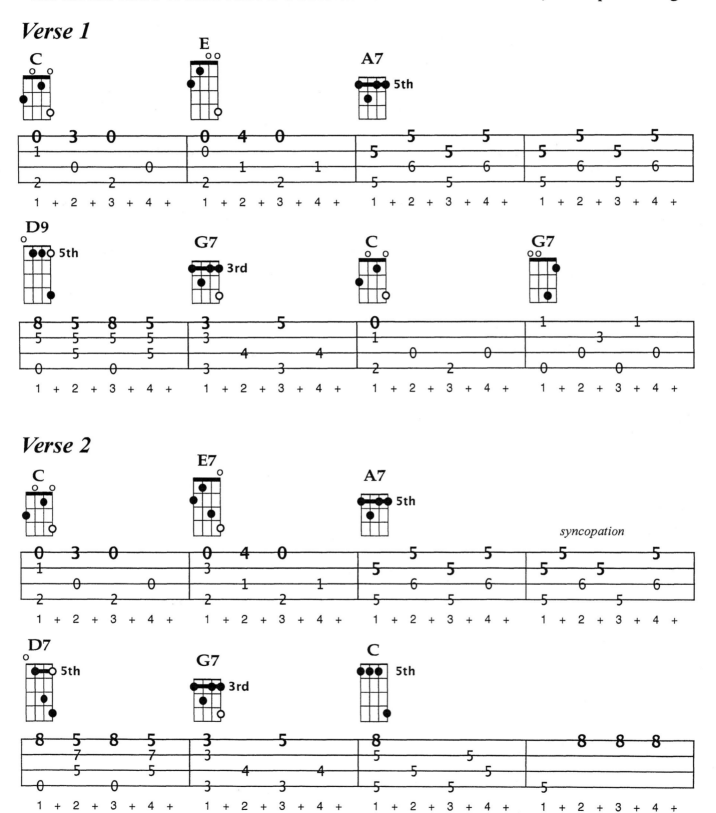

Bridge

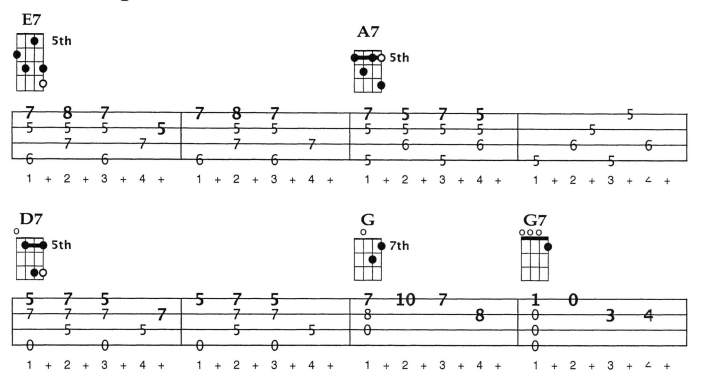

Verse 3

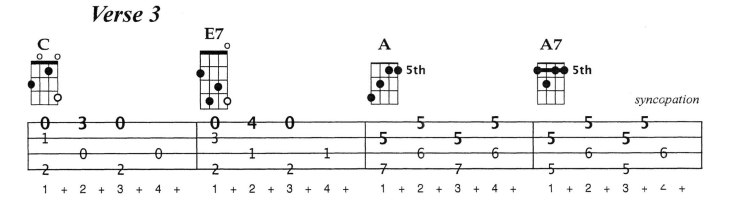

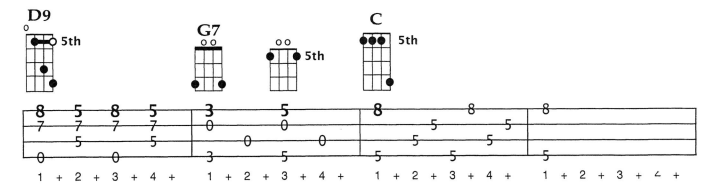

Beyond the Major and the Minor Chords
a.k.a. Chords of Color

You certainly should know something about Chord Qualities other than
the straight Major, Minor and Seventh. You know about triads, the **1 - 3 - 5's**,
and you know about one kind of **1 - 3 - 5 - 7** quadrad, the Seventh chord.
But there are other scale degrees, like the **2nd, 4th, 6th, 9th**, etc.,
that can be combined with these triads and quadrads
to make beautiful music together.

To figure out these other Chord Qualities, we need to start with the Major Scale
of whatever the **Root Note** of the chord happens to be, then calculate from there.
Some of these you've seen before, but now you see them in chordal context.
For some of these chords, it's impossible to work in all the notes we'd like,
so I'll just give you the shapes that are the most practical and sound best.

Here are the Chord Qualities we are interested in:

Major. Structure: **1 - 3 - 5**. Happy. The Three Stooges: "Hello, hello, hello!"

Minor. Structure: **1 - b3 - 5**. Sad, dark, forlorn, the war chord, the scary chord.

sus2 = Suspended 2nd. Structure: **1 - 2 - 3 - 5**. A Major sound that leaves you hanging.

sus4 = Suspended 4th. Structure: **1 - 4 - 5**. Also hanging, but would clash with the **3rd**.

5 = Power Chord. Structure: **1 - 5**. That's it. No **3rd**. All angles & edges & muscle.

6 = Major 6th. Structure: **1 - 3 - 5 - 6**. Contemplative, breezy, good ending chord.

m6 = Minor 6th. Structure: **1 - b3 - 5 - 6**. Sad but expectant. Sounds almost pushy.

7 = (Dominant) 7th. Structure: **1 - 3 - 5 - b7**. A Major sound at heart, but bluesy and edgy.

ma7 = Major 7th. Structure: **1 - 3 - 5 - 7**. A happy, jazzy sound. Can sub for Major.

m7 = Minor 7th. Structure: **1 - b3 - 5 - b7**. Not as dark as a pure Minor. Bittersweet.

9 = (Dominant) 9th. Structure: **1 - 3 - 5 - 7 - 9**. An edgy, jazzy sound. Can sub for Dom 7.

11 = (Dominant) 11th. Structure: **1 - 3 - 5 - 7 - 9 - 11**. Also called **sus7**; suspended, edgier **sus4**.

13 = (Dominant) 13th. Structure: **1 - 3 - 5 - 7 - 9 - 11 - 13**. All the notes! Complex and rich.

dim7 = Diminished 7th. Structure: **1 - b3 - b5 - bb7**. *Much* pushier than Dom 7.

G Chord Qualities from the G Scale

87

I just want to run you through the whole process ONCE, using the G Major Scale. You remember the **G Major Scale**? *Pisces, rather tall, passable dancer?*

G	A	B	C	D	E	F#
1	2	3	4	5	6	7

(1) *Below Left*. Take the 7 notes and lay them out along the G string, the 3rd string, so you can SEE the structure of the Whole-steps and Half-steps in the scale.

(2) *Middle*. Substitute the scale degrees (the numbers) for the letters, so we'll have a common language between keys. *Throw in the b3rds and b7th---we'll need 'em.* This is very nice, but it takes a lot more than one string to make a chord, so.....

(3) *Right*. Fill in all the rest of the scale degrees on the other three strings. Now the structure is more complex (it's a mess), but we can make chords from clumps of notes that reflect the different Chord Qualities and can be fingered.

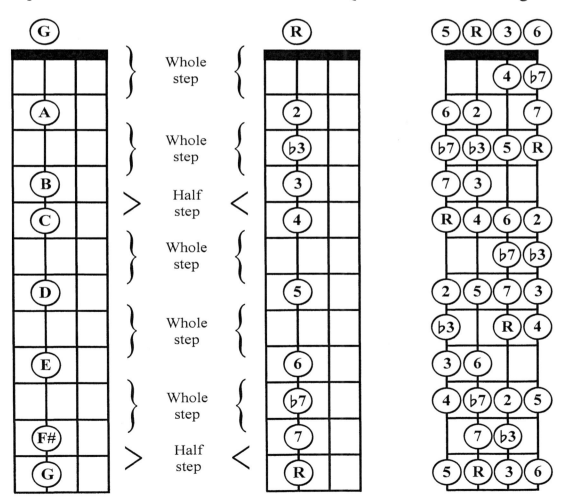

All Kindza G Chords

Now, I don't care whether or not you can plow through that last diagram and generate all those different kindza **G** chords (if you want to just eat the fish or reel them in yourself). Actually, it's really not so bad. You might want to trace several of the chords below back through the process, just to convince yourself that it's the whole truth and nothing but.

Okay. All these suspended chords in the first line like to resolve to the Major chord.

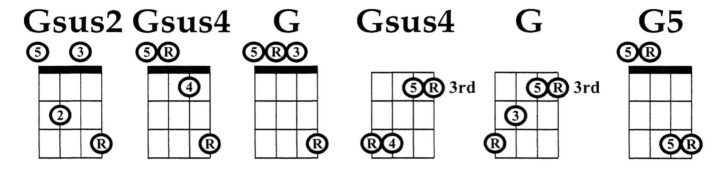

G5 is pretty common, **Gm6** not so much. **G6** makes a good ending chord (Beatles' *Help*), and **Gma7** is a good substitution for **G** in a jazz or pop music context (*Sunny, Misty*).

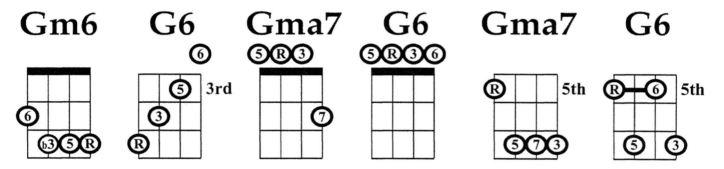

The first 3 chords below make a nice Jazz Turnaround (**2m7 - 57 - 1ma7**) in the **Key of F**. The **Fma7** is new to you.....pretty. The terms "9th, 11th and 13th" chords need explaining. The notes are actually the **2nd**, **4th** and **6th**, respectively, but whenever there is also a **7th** present in the chord, you bump them up an octave and call them **9th, 11th** and **13th** chords. These **complex** dominant chords resolve nicely in the **5 - 1** progression to the **1 chord**, C.

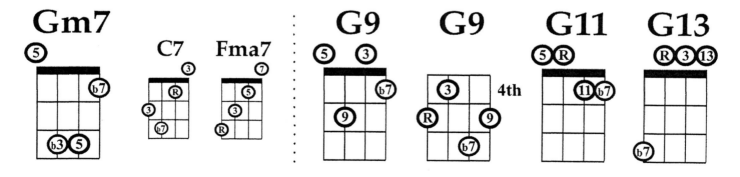

C Chord Qualities from the C Scale

C Scale Degrees

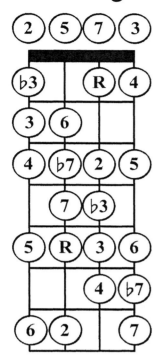

Again, don't be too concerned about navigating your way through the **C** scale degree diagram to the left. I just want you to see that I'm not making this up, that these clusters of notes we use to form the chords come from *somewhere*.

Csus2 is not very satisfying, but if you ever need it, you got it. The **Csus4** needs both **4ths**; we can't let either one of those **3rds** from the **C** chord ring over the **4th**. Truly bad.

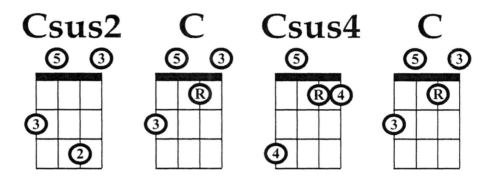

The **Cm** near the nut is okay, but it isn't fun to play; try the one at the 3rd fret, or **Cm6** or **Cm7**. And there isn't a good **Cma7** near the nut (sounds like **Em**), but the 5th fret has good **G** shape versions of the **C7** and **Cma7** chords.

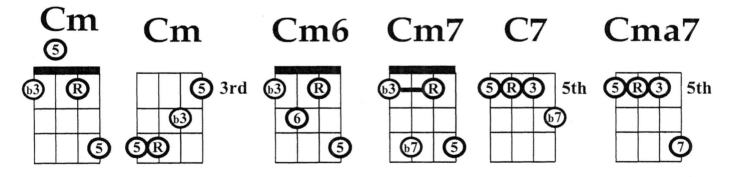

*[You are not going to like this, but there's a **C9** chord that has the same shape as **Gm6**. The difference is that the **Gm6** chord has the chord tones 6 - b3 - 5 - R, while **C9** has the **same notes** labeled as 3 - b7 - 9 - 5. Both chords are still spelled **G - Bb - D - G**. It is the **Root Note** that you count from that is responsible for the difference. The same notes just function differently in the respective chords. We'll keep running into situations like this, so I wanted to acknowledge it, but I won't keep bringing it up.]*

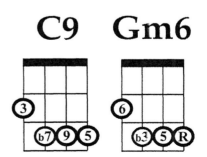

D Chord Qualities from the D Scale

D Scale Degrees

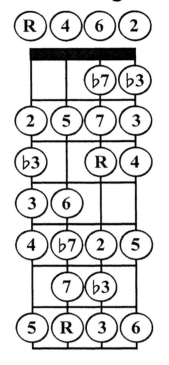

The following 4 chords sound great, in sequence, during a **5 chord** section of a **5 - 1** progression to a G chord in the **Key of G**.

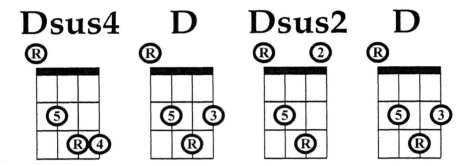

All these **D** chords sound particularly strong, because they have the **D Root Note** in the bass, a very solid foundation.

A new Chord Quality has snuck in below, the **Major 9th**. It's a more dissonant, open-sounding version of **Dma7**. James Taylor uses this chord a lot on the guitar.

Again, any of those complex dominant **D** chords will resolve quite agreeably in a **5 - 1** progression to the **1 chord**, G.

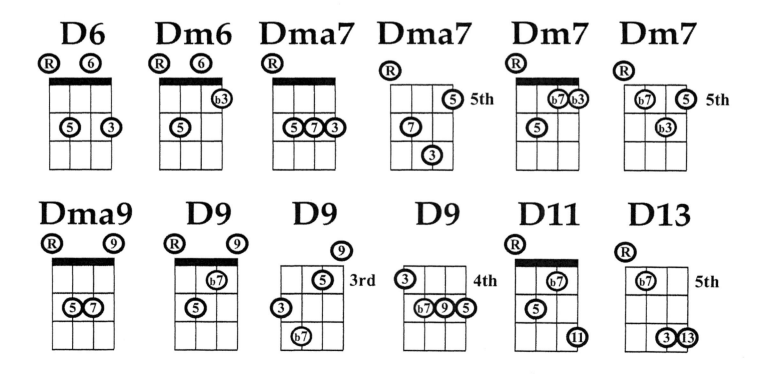

Assuming you grok the process we've been applying, here's just a catalog of Chord Qualities for the final two of our *C-A-G-E-D* Chord Families, **A** and **E**. Same sorts of sultry sounds you've been hearing in the sections on **G**, **C** and **D**. Play with them, see which ones you like, you might use them some day.

A Chord Qualities from the A Scale

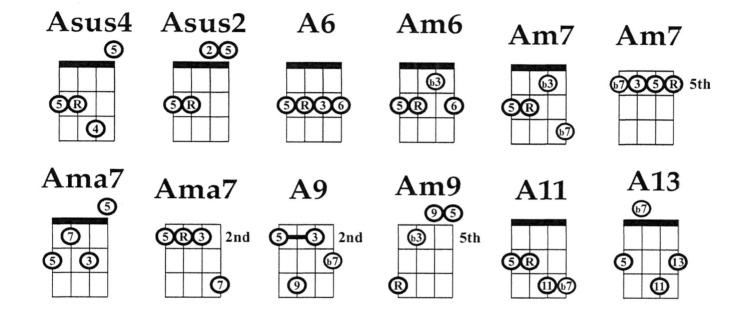

E Chord Qualities from the E Scale

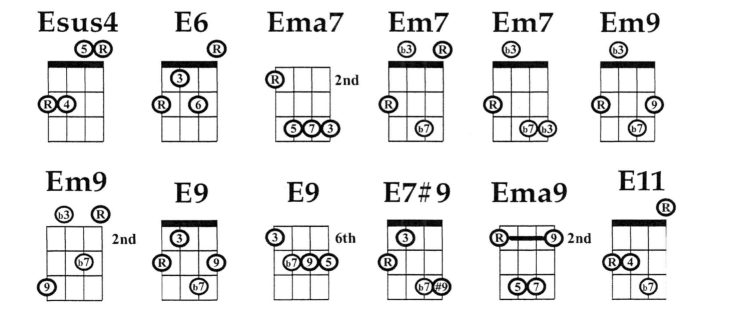

Diminished Chords

Infrequently you will see a Diminished chord on a song sheet, or, more likely, a **Diminished Seventh** chord (**dim7**). These guys are extremely dissonant, almost belligerent, which makes them excellent passing chords, that you can't WAIT to put behind you! Well, I exaggerate a bit, but they certainly are chords that say, "Don't ignore me."

Most people skip them, but they aren't hard to play and they do add some pizzazz. Oddly enough, there is only *one basic chord shape* that is required to play all 12 **dim7s**. You take the letter name of the chord, find that note on the neck, and make sure that one of your fingers covers that note within the chord shape, which is a rhombus.

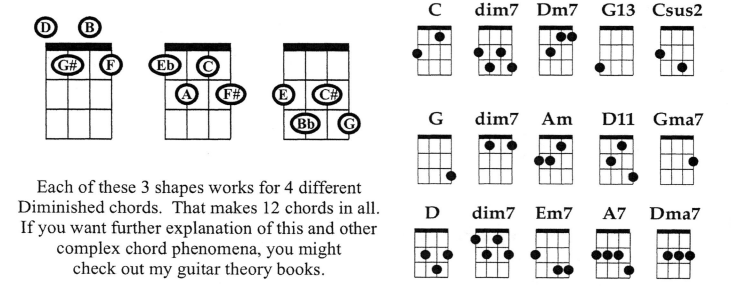

Each of these 3 shapes works for 4 different Diminished chords. That makes 12 chords in all. If you want further explanation of this and other complex chord phenomena, you might check out my guitar theory books.

Some F-type Chord Qualities

F is a pretty prominent chord in the **Key of C**, so here are some nice variations you can use to keep your **F** chords smelling fresh, like springtime in the Poconos.

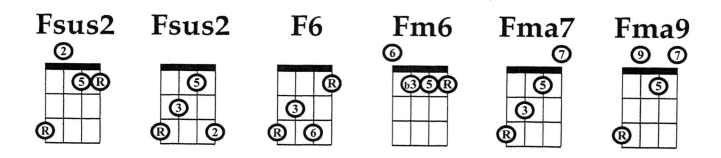

Rhythm Changes in the Keys of C, G and D

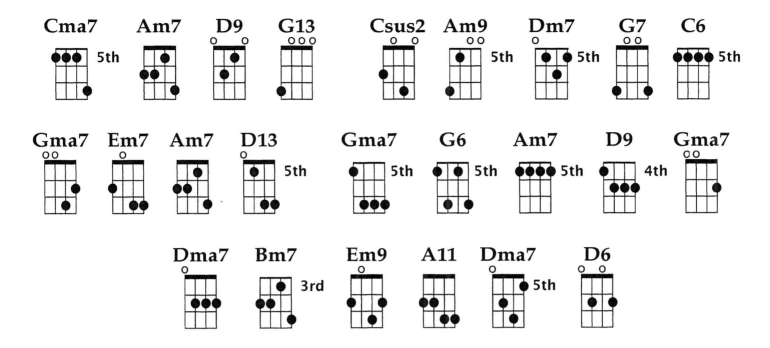

America the Beautiful in Three Keys

Key of C

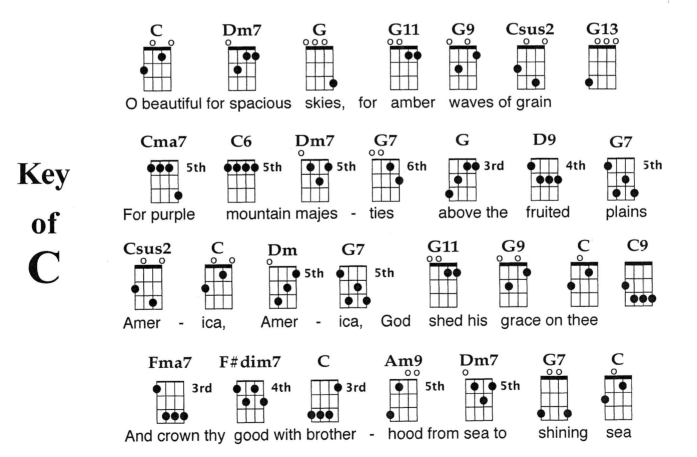

Key of G

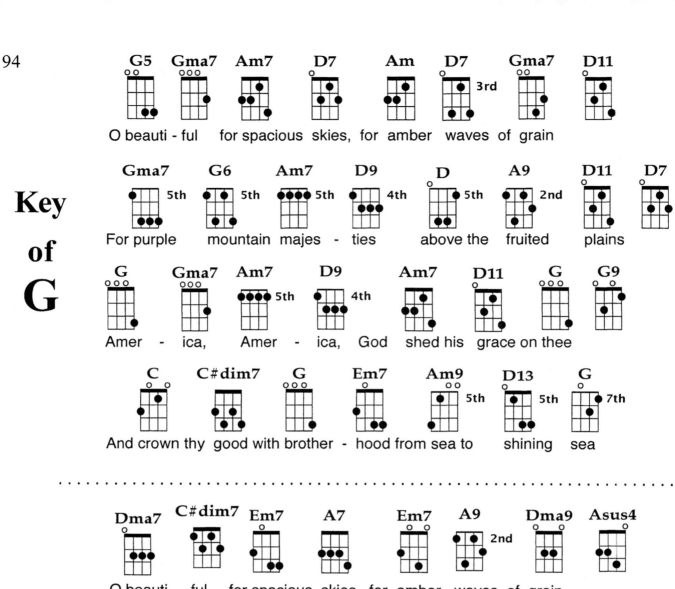

Key of D

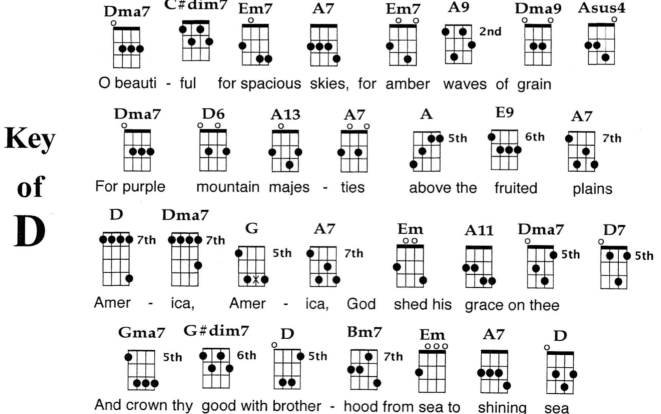

Minor Keys

They aren't as common as Major Keys, but you will doubtless run into **Minor Keys**. You might have thought that they would be, more or less, sad versions of Major Keys, and you would have been spot on. You might *also* have thought that, for example, the **Keys of A** and **Am** would be closely related, but that would be more spot off.

The **Key of A** has 3 sharps while the **Key of Am** is the *Relative Minor Key to C*, so it has no accidentals at all. And remember that the *Major* **Keys of C** and **A** have not a single chord in common. So there.

Still, there are two *differences* between the **Keys of C** and **Am**. First, the **1 chord** is now **Am**; you shift the rest of the chords around on a conveyer belt to assign the numbers:

Am	Bdim	C	Dm	Em	F	G
1	2	3	4	5	6	7

So we still talk about the **1 - 4 - 5** chords, but now they all have a Minor Chord Quality: The **1 chord** is **Am**, the **4 chord** is **Dm** and the **5 chord** is **Em**, which is all *parallel* to the **Key of A**, but still *in* the **Key of C**. Beyond the **1 - 4 - 5**, I think it's unnecessary, even confusing, to refer to the other common chords, **C**, **F** and **G**, by their new numbers; I just consider them to be the three Major chords in the **Key of Am**.

The second (potential) difference between the **Keys of C** and **Am** has to do with the **5 chord** in the **Key of Am**, which is **Em**. The problem is that we'd like to have a more *dominant* sound in the **5 chord** than the **Em** provides; after all, it's supposed to have a sort of *push*, and **Em** doesn't. So what *they* decided to do was to substitute either the **E** or **E7** chord for **Em**, and that seems to slake our thirst for power. Try it: Play the **1 - 4 - 5 - 1**, first as **Am - Dm - Em - Am**, then as **Am - Dm - *E7* - Am**. *The second one resolves from the 5 chord to the 1 chord with greater conviction.* So here are the Chord Families for the **Keys of Em** and **Dm**, with **5₇ chords**:

Em	F#dim	G	A	B7	C	D
1	2	3	4	5	6	7

Dm	Edim	F	Gm	A7	Bb	C
1	2	3	4	5	6	7

Examples in Minor Keys

Both of the following songs, *We Three Kings* on this page and *God Rest Ye Merry, Gentlemen* on the next, start off firmly within the bounds of the three Chord Families, **Am**, **Em** and **Dm**, but then they begin dancing back and forth with the Relative Major Keys, **C**, **G** and **F**, using those *Major 1 - 4 - 5's*. Very interesting.

```
Am              E7    Am              E7      Am
We three kings of orient are,   bearing gifts we traverse a-far

Am      G      C                    Dm    E7    Am
Field and fountain,  moor and mountain,  following yonder star

G  G7  C            F     C              F      C
O,   o,    star of wonder, star of night, star with royal beauty bright

Am     G     F    G7    C            F      C
Westward leading, still pro-ceeding, guide us to thy perfect light


Em              B7    Em              B7      Em
We three kings of orient are,   bearing gifts we traverse a-far

Em      D      G                    Am    B7    Em
Field and fountain,  moor and mountain,  following yonder star

D  D7  G            C     G              C      G
O,   o,    star of wonder, star of night, star with royal beauty bright

Em     D     C    D7    G            C      G
Westward leading, still pro-ceeding, guide us to thy perfect light


Dm              A7    Dm              A7      Dm
We three kings of orient are,   bearing gifts we traverse a-far

Dm      C      F                    Gm    A7    Dm
Field and fountain,  moor and mountain,  following yonder star

C  C7  F            Bb    F              Bb     F
O,   o,    star of wonder, star of night, star with royal beauty bright

Dm     C     Bb   C7    F            Bb     F
Westward leading, still pro-ceeding, guide us to thy perfect light
```

```
        Am     E7    Am            Dm              E7
God rest ye merry, gentlemen, let nothing you dis-may
     Am     E7     Am       Dm              E7
Re-member Christ our Savior was born on Christmas Day
   Dm     G7     C     E7          Am     D7    G7
To save us all from Satan's power when we were gone a-stray
     C    F     E7          F               G7
O, tid - ings of comfort and joy, comfort and joy
     C    F     E7          Am
O, tid - ings of comfort and joy


        Em     B7    Em            Am              B7
God rest ye merry, gentlemen, let nothing you dis-may
     Em     B7     Em       Am              B7
Re-member Christ our Savior was born on Christmas Day
   Am     D7     G     B7          Em     A7    D7
To save us all from Satan's power when we were gone a-stray
     G    C     B7          C               D7
O, tid - ings of comfort and joy, comfort and joy
     G    C     B7          Em
O, tid - ings of comfort and joy


        Dm     A7    Dm            Gm              A7
God rest ye merry, gentlemen, let nothing you dis-may
     Dm     A7     Dm       Gm              A7
Re-member Christ our Savior was born on Christmas Day
   Gm     C7     F     A7          Dm     G7    C7
To save us all from Satan's power when we were gone a-stray
     F    Bb    A7          Bb              C7
O, tid - ings of comfort and joy, comfort and joy
     F    Bb    A7          Dm
O, tid - ings of comfort and joy
```

Intro to Single String Playing

So far, we really haven't been concerned with "playing scales" in this book. We've used the Major Scale to generate our Chord Families, and all the melodies that we used in the chord/melody arrangements come from Major Scales.

But **single string playing** is something that the Advancing Uker should know something about, so let's spend our last few cherished moments together poking at it with a pointed stick. See if we can get a rise out of it.

If there's enough interest from readers, I can publish a supplemental booklet that will go into more depth on playing and improvising with scales.

Take a look at these Fretboard Diagrams and the accompanying Tab:

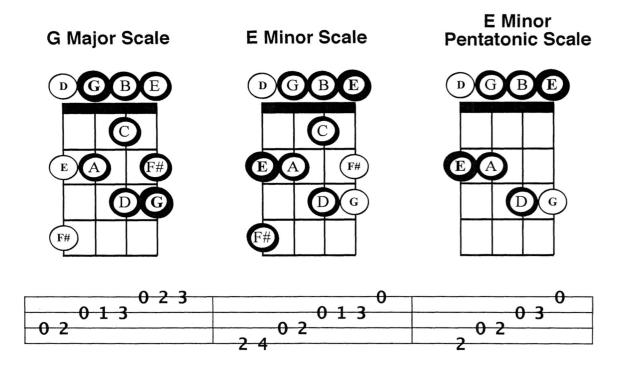

In the **G Major Scale**, the notes in the bolder circles represent one octave, and those are the notes shown in the Tab. As you know, the **Em** chord is the Relative Minor of **G**. Well, the **Em** *Scale* is the Relative Minor of the **G** *Scale*: same notes, but now the E note is the **Root Note** of the scale, and when you play from E to E, the sound is *Minor*.

Finally we have the **E Minor Pentatonic Scale**, which eliminates 2 notes from the Minor Scale, leaving 5 (penta=5) more widely spaced scale degrees.
This is the scale to start with when improvising blues lead parts.

First, some practice playing the full **G Major Scale**, including *Ode to Joy to the World*. Several notes drop below the lower **Root Note** (onto the 4th string) into the octave below:

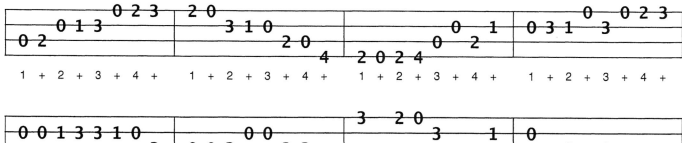

Next, the full **Em Scale** (rest ye easy):

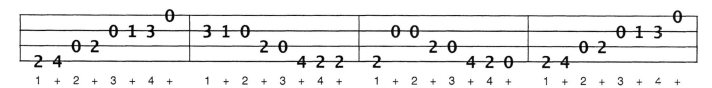

Now comes the fun scale, the **Em Pentatonic**. You can just noodle around in it, especially when someone else is playing a 12-bar blues. ***You can't make a mistake!*** And look, I gave you an extra note at the 5th fret, 1st string, that you can slide to (**S**):

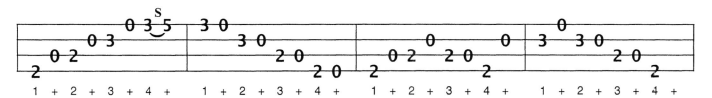

Now, I mean it about the noodling: You can play any of these notes in any order and be technically correct. Even if it's incoherent. It's like language in that you can say any of the words in this paragraph in any order and it's still English, even if it's Gibberish. You need to learn where these notes are located and just try different combinations to see what sounds coherent. Some noodling:

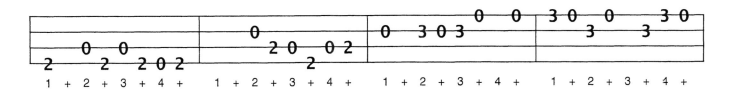

It ain't great art, but it's a start.

100

Just as there are 5 chord shapes around the neck, there are 5 corresponding *scale* shapes, and this first one is the **Em** shape. See the **Em** chord embedded in the scale?

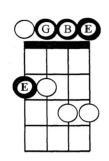

Well, since you know about ***C-A-G-E-D***, you know that the next shape up the neck is the **Dm** shape. You can see the scale shape and the embedded **Dm** chord shape to the right:

One way to move from the **Em** shape to the **Dm** shape is by sliding up and down along the 3rd string, thus:

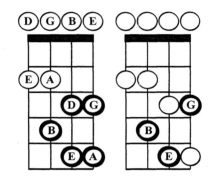

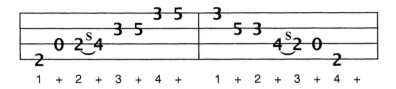

Way up the neck there is another fun scale shape to try, the **Gm** shape (see the chord shape as well, to the right). Try the first two measures of the Tab, down the scale and back up. See the E note at the 9th fret? *That's the very same note with the same pitch as the open 1st string E, making it a perfect segue, or wormhole, for jumping between the higher and lower shapes, as in Measure 3:*

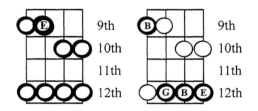

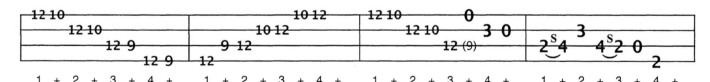

Let's finish with a 12-bar blues pattern in the **Key of E**---this is the accompaniment part to the notes you are noodling with. (Pinch these.)

Tempus fugit. Thanks for reading. Contact me any time!

Aloha 'oe!

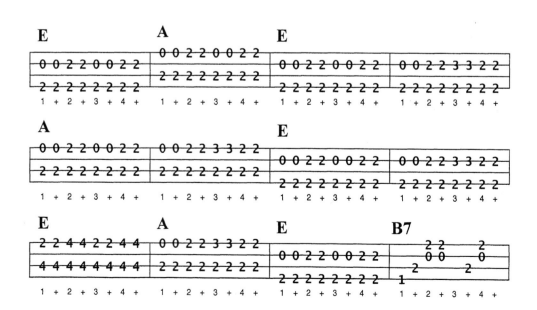